WEDNESDAY WANDERS

A light-hearted Account of Weekly Adventures along the Footpaths of Southeast England

By

Mark Bowden

Grosvenor House
Publishing Limited

This book is published by
Grosvenor House Publishing Ltd
Link House
140 The Broadway, Tolworth, Surrey, KT6 7HT.
www.grosvenorhousepublishing.co.uk

A CIP record for this book
is available from the British Library

ISBN 978-1-80381-746-0
eBook ISBN 978-1-80381-747-7

Contents

Introduction   v

Chapter 1   The London LOOP   1

Chapter 2   The North Downs Way   21

Chapter 3   The Ridgeway Path   41

Chapter 4   The Icknield Way Path   49

Chapter 5   The Chiltern Way   63

Chapter 6   The Greensand Way   83

Chapter 7   The Hertfordshire Way   97

Introduction

The relentless headwind is trying its best, but has failed yet again to prevent me from reaching the top of an impossibly steep climb. This is the third or fourth; I've lost count. Suddenly, that same wind has turned ally, acting as a brake to the equally steep descent. This clifftop path is diverted inland for a few hundred yards in a few places where the eroded chalk is considered too unstable. To my left is the ever-present traffic noise from the A20 trunk road making its way to Dover, as am I. There is some reprieve from the noise and the elements when the trail runs through short corridors of gorse bush. But lingering in the bushes seems unwise, so the peace and tranquillity last only a few seconds.

I was on the final few miles of the North Downs Way, the first of my weekly long-distance-path adventures. I had set out on the first stage on a wet Wednesday in November, armed with an Ordnance Survey (OS) map and a naïve belief that waymarkers alone would suffice. This final section was completed the following April, a week before Easter. I'd learned a lot, was fitter, and, hopefully, a little wiser.

This book contains an account of that first long-distance path, plus the six others that followed. Taken from the write-ups I'd produced for a few loyal Facebook friends, they tell of success and folly, people met, and places visited. There are a few repetitive themes: early morning trains, coffee and cake, navigational follies, steep hills, muddy footpaths, and Antarctic explorers. But I have also tried to convey something of the beautiful vistas and the joy of walking a thousand miles on some of south-east England's finest long-distance trails.

Chapter One

The London LOOP

The London Outer Orbital Path, or London LOOP, was not my first long-distance path. It was the latest. The semi-urban route might lack the remote countryside and magnificent views encountered on the preceding walks, but it was full of interest and many surprises as the path threads around the borderland of Greater London and the Home Counties. And I felt it would make a fitting start to this account of my adventures.

Yet I was reluctant to do the walk. During my 44 years as a service engineer, I visited most parts of south-east England. The majority of my calls, though, were in and around the capital, and I was anxious to explore further afield in retirement. The need for a project over the wintertime and reading some good reviews won me over. The LOOP starts on the south bank of the Thames Estuary and makes its way clockwise for 150 miles around London. There is some road walking but also an abundance of parkland, riverside paths, and open countryside. A cleverly conceived and highly enjoyable walk.

Erith to Petts Wood: 6 October 2022 (16 miles)

Stepping out from the rather grand railway station, you can understand why Erith, perched on the south bank of the Thames Estuary, once had ambitions as a resort. It's hard to believe we're still in London, and although it might be my imagination, there's a hint of sea breeze in the air. I know Erith has a riverside garden and pier, which I'm yet to see, but first, it's coffee. The town centre is almost deserted at 8.00 am, with most shops still firmly shuttered. The only activity is the stall traders unloading produce from delivery vans. Thankfully, I can still find somewhere for coffee and a bun to launch my new adventure.

1

The first LOOP sign I find is in the Riverside Gardens. It's wonky, but points in generally the right direction, and without an official start point, it will suffice. Now for a reality check. I soon discover that it's not deckchairs and amusement arcades that drive this town but the surrounding and encroaching industry. Much of it seems to be metal recycling. It will take four miles to shake off its noisy presence.

Skirting around Morrison's car park, then an uncomfortable mile along a narrow pavement, with the noise and fumes of a constant stream of lorries serving the numerous trading estates. I'm relieved when the road runs out, and I'm on the path leading across Crayford Marshes and onto Crayford Ness. It's here that the Darent flows into the Thames. The corner where the rivers meet has a wild look: one small bush bravely standing alone among an expanse of tussocky grass. On a windy day, it would not be a place to linger. The brutal crash of metal on metal from the recycling plants still rings loudly across the scene. Turning away from the estuary, the route follows the Darent and then the River Cray to Bexley. But it's not without negotiating busy road junctions and crossing several railway bridges. One is left in no doubt suburbia is close at hand.

After leaving Bexley, things feel much more rural as the route enters Foots Cray Meadows with its generous tract of Green Belt running either side of the Cray. Reaching the town of Foots Cray and having walked 11 miles, it's time for lunch. I'm a bit weary and almost settle for a bench beside the busy traffic lights. Rejecting that thirty seconds after sitting down, I manage a few more hundred yards to a small park behind the allotments. Wishing I'd stopped earlier, by the river. The afternoon's highlights are undoubtedly Scadbury Park Nature Reserve and Petts Wood. Noise from road and rail links seldom disappears entirely, but at least we've left the scrapyards behind.

The expansive Petts Wood contains a hidden gem close to my heart. Leaving the main path, I fight through the undergrowth like Speck and Burton searching for the source of the Nile (or so I pretended). And suddenly, a clearing appeared and, with it, the object of my search. An obelisk, about five-feet high, with a sundial on one side and an intriguing inscription on the other, 'This wood was purchased by public subscription as a tribute to WILLIAM WILLETT, the untiring advocate of Summer Time.' In the early 20th century, he harangued the government to introduce daylight saving (now BST). A young Winston Churchill took up the cause, but it would take World War One to make it law, and we have not looked back (or is it forward?) since. There is a pub in Petts Wood named 'The Daylight Inn' in Willett's honour.

This will be a somewhat different challenge from my recent, remoter ventures – for example, meeting people. A friendly lot, they seem too, which is nice. But whatever happens, I've started, so I'll finish.

Petts Wood to South Croydon: 26 October 2022 (13 miles)

Following an enforced three-week Covid break, it was good to get back on the trail today. However, my first steps are tentative as I contemplate the fine line between adventure and folly. A line I have occasionally crossed but must avoid today. The refrain to 'Just be sensible and stop when you're tired' is still ringing in my ears.

There's so much glorious countryside on today's walk that it's hard to believe we are still in Greater London, Bromley, to be more precise. Much of it was once in Kent, and one could understand any fellow feeling with those who mourn the loss of Middlesex.

Although the day was not without its busy roads and housing estates, there were also several miles of woodland paths and expansive green parkland. Much of the latter once formed the large estates of the wealthy, perhaps wanting to establish their presence near, but not too near, the capital. One is High Elms Country Park, now a council-owned nature reserve. The Italian-style mansion burnt down long ago. An Eton Fives court is one structure that has survived for over 170 years and is virtually unscathed. A bizarrely shaped three-sided concrete playing area, not unlike a squash court but with the addition of hazards such as a buttress encroaching on the playing area. Invented by a school famous for producing prime ministers. It has a lot to answer for.

Keeping with the political theme, it's only a short distance until we meet another country estate, Holwood. Climbing a path to a hilltop where to the right, and fenced off to the general public, is a stone bench. To the left and slightly downhill is a forlorn tree that has all but been destroyed by lightning, just one broken branch pointing skywards. And the significance of both the bench and the tree? It's the spot where Wilberforce and Pitt the Younger first discussed the abolition of slavery. Three walkers have stopped to read the inscription and we talk for a few minutes. 'Where are you heading?' they ask. I tell them I hope to get to Banstead but having been unwell for a couple of weeks, I may finish sooner. I don't share the nature of my illness. They walk on, but I linger for a few more minutes to appreciate the spot and drink some water.

A third and tenuous political link is found shortly after descending what we might call Wilberforce Hill (although it's not). And that link is Caesar's Well. It's the source of the River Ravensbourne on its epic 11 mile journey to meet the Thames at Deptford. An attractive circular, brick construction pools and channels the emerging spring to a series of three large ponds whose output becomes the river. As I follow the path around the first pond, or lake really, I see my trio of new friends sitting at a picnic table at the top of an embankment. They wave enthusiastically, which is nice.

Like many open spaces around outer London, Wickham Common is owned and maintained by The City of London Corporation. Invariably characterised by imposingly large black notice boards, on the back of which are written so many by-laws that it must surely be the reason the boards are so big. Number 12 catches my eye and includes the following prohibitions: 'no placing clothes or other things on the trees' and 'no shaking, beating or brushing carpets or mats'. I feel like bringing a mat to shake in defiance.

A lovely walk through Threehalfpenny Wood brought me to Addington Hill and a stiff climb to the concrete viewing point. From here are great views towards Croydon and much of south London. This includes the Crystal Palace television transmitter, which I'm particularly excited about.

As it was a being-sensible day, when I got to the bottom of the hill, I caught a tram from Coombe Lane station into Croydon (and thence a train home). Work often took me to the town, and it might be interesting to see it again. To some, Croydonisation may be a pejorative term, but it's not so bad a place.

South Croydon to South Coulsdon: 1 November 2022 (12 miles)

Today's section of the LOOP looked promising, with its woodland paths and green spaces twisting around suburbia like a cunning snake.

Happy Valley and Farthing Downs sounded especially spectacular. But it didn't quite work out as planned.

The train to Croydon and the tram to the start went ok, as did the first couple of miles through parkland and a nature reserve. A relatively dull and chilly day, but, as yet, no rain.

Then I got to Selsdon Wood. A steep climb through this ancient woodland during which I got lost, it started to rain (just as I had the map spread on the ground), and the irregular heartbeat that has plagued me for several years made an unwelcome appearance. And finally, on a narrow and uneven descent, I slipped on an exposed tree root and began sliding downhill feet first. Grabbing a nearby sapling, I just about managed to arrest my fall. Sitting for a minute for some existential pondering before taking a quick selfie to check for damage and, back up on my feet, carefully I carried on.

Now on firmer ground and with a brief show of sunshine, life seemed much better. My heart wasn't right but should cope as long as there were no more hills. Of course, there were. But for now, the pleasant and gentle path descending into Hamsey Green was trouble-free.

I had meant to buy something for lunch when I got to Croydon but forgot and tried to find a convenience store in the parade of shops here. However, not wanting to go too much out of my way, I only got as far as the hairdressers and the undertakers before giving up. Oh well, I had a flask of tea.

The route continued on the far side of the road, over a railway bridge, and along a dead end that slowly rose to the base of Kenley Common. The way to the top is via a short but steep zig-zag path. This usually means it's too steep to go straight up. I'd normally embrace the challenge, but still feeling far from well, it was a horrible prospect. I paused before attempting the task, looked back across the valley, and was astonished at what I saw. Looming high above the recently crossed main road was a wide expanse of chalk cliff. Who would have believed it, the White Cliffs of Bromley? A remnant of 19th-century mining activity.

But I can't put off the moment any longer to start my 'serious climb' as the guidebook has it. Short it may have been, but by the time I staggered onto the somewhat bleak common, I was in a bad way. It took several minutes until I felt ready to head along the woodland path that skirts the right-hand edge of the plateau. Further on, a lesser path dives through the trees to follow close to what was Kenley Airfield in World War Two.

The LOOP drops down to visit Old Coulsdon before entering Happy Valley. This is the title of the first novel by one of my favourite authors, Patrick White, set in the Australian outback. It wasn't a very happy valley. Nor, I suspect, is the TV series one set in West Yorkshire, judging by the trailers. But at least this one made me happy, following a level and firm path. Passing a bench, I decided to stop and enjoy my flask of tea.

Happy Valley leads onto Farthing Downs and has a view over the houses of South Coulsdon, before the track drops into the town near the station. This is a convenient stopping point as the trail crosses the platform bridge. But before considering a train home, I need food. Nothing in the immediate vicinity, so I head towards the town centre. Sandwiches would do, but I fancy a bit more and search the high street until I find a café where I order sausage, egg and chips.

It wasn't award-winning cuisine, and the large-screen TV just a few feet away showing a programme about vets, with rather too graphic scenes of a donkey being castrated, was a little off-putting. But hungry, tired, and a bit fed up with the spirit-versus-body thing, it was terrific. I even had a second cup of tea.

South Coulsdon to Kingston:
15 November 2022 (16 miles)

If I asked you what London is famous for, I suspect lavender growing would be pretty low on the list. However, it was a thriving industry during the 18th and 19th centuries. And it's been revived at Mayfield Lavender Fields in Sutton. Complete with a visitor centre and gift shop, *Time Out* rates it London's number one lavender venue, and the LOOP passes right through the middle. Although, being November, there is no 'Purple Haze' to flood the senses, just a grey carpet of summer memories.

Much of today's walk is in Surrey, a county which someone has calculated is 2.65% golf course. I only encountered one today, which went surprisingly well by my standards. In fact, it's a good day all round as some early dampness gives way to a modestly bright day, and I have no repeat of the health problems that plagued my last outing.

After a reasonably long road section through South Ewell, the trail enters Nonsuch Park. Apparently, it was given that name after someone exclaimed, 'There is nonsuch in all Europe.' It has a mansion which I don't visit because the LOOP doesn't. The trail only crosses the park's south-west corner, and there's no time for diversions.

This vast space was a hunting ground for Henry VIII, which required the destruction of the village of Cuddington to accommodate it. We do pass where his palace was, now no more, and the foundations of a banqueting house for the king to entertain his guests. Chasing defenceless animals around the countryside must have been hungry work.

But we can't leave Nonsuch without mentioning 'The Ghost Roads'– two parallel concrete tracks that run through the woods on the park's southern boundary. Several theories exist about why, when, and by whom they were built. One idea is that they were for an atmospheric railway, i.e., that used air pressure to drive it. Another thought is that they were built during World War Two as a track to a secret bunker or an emergency landing strip for aircraft. The most plausible but prosaic theory is that it was a new road abandoned at the outbreak of war. I think it was for landing alien spaceships. Maybe they are still with us. Who knows, maybe I'm an alien?

The second half of the route mostly follows the Hogsmill River on its six-mile journey from the source at Ewell to the Thames at Kingston. Little more than a stream at first, it swells to a broad and fast-flowing river as it anticipates the end of its short journey. The riverside paths make walking easy and enjoyable with only the occasional 'sticky patch'. I'm sure more stickiness will follow in the coming months.

It's raining when I arrive in Kingston, and I want to get to the station as quickly as possible. But only after visiting an iconic art installation, 12 red telephone boxes, stacked like a falling row of dominoes frozen in time. I wonder if this is a nod to Kingston upon Hull with its cream white telephone boxes (some now Grade ll listed apparently). But probably not.

Kingston to Hayes: 23 November 2022 (13 miles)

Standing on the top balcony of the Bentall's Shopping Centre, the already impressive space looked even more splendid in its Christmas livery, and the numerous escalators and winding staircases gave the impression of a giant 3D snakes and ladders game – Yuletide edition. What fun that would be. It was 9.00 am, and few people had voluntarily ventured out on this dismally wet morning. But I needed coffee after a fraught journey to Kingston.

Clapham Junction at rush hour had lived up to its reputation as the personification of a frantically busy space – people rushing like ants in a nest through the walkways that connect its 17 platforms, although stopping short of exchanging pheromones at each turning. Add a miserable half hour waiting on an exposed platform at Willesden Junction station, where the bedraggled passengers were offered as a sacrifice to the elemental gods, and you might excuse a soft start to my adventure.

Much of today's route could be described as the Clapham Junction of the London LOOP, a frenetic corner of south-west London that includes several major roads and a motorway, usually enough of a distraction on their own, today they are eclipsed by another presence – Heathrow Airport.

Firstly, I must tear myself away from the warm, dry coffee shop and head for Kingston Bridge. On the other side is Bushy Park, adjacent to Hampton Court and yet another hunting ground for Henry VIII. It covers a vast area that will take 30 minutes to cross, even at a fast, non-lingering pace.

Long after Henry's hunting parties had departed, Charles I took a more ascetic view of things by commissioning the Longford River, a 12-mile canal built to bring water to the palace and to supply the various fountains and lakes in the park. Then came William III, who commissioned the ostentatious Chestnut Avenue, a mile-long grand approach to the palace from the north. One further fact that would most likely have all three monarchs turning in their graves is that Bushy Park is where the Park Run originated.

After taking the exit to Teddington, there is a long stretch along roads until, with some relief, the river Crane is met. For about four miles, the LOOP follows the river wherever it can, offering some respite from the busy roads. I see more of Hounslow Heath than planned when I miss a sharp turn that would have reunited me with the Crane. An unexpectedly wild place amid so much turmoil and, apparently, once a dangerous place frequented by highwaymen in wait for travellers leaving the capital. They have long since gone, thankfully.

In the 18th Century, the initial five mile triangulation baseline for the Board of Ordnance (later the Ordnance Survey) ran across the heath. This allowed the mapping of the whole of Britain to be achieved with extortionary accuracy. In an undemonstrative act of homage, I tap the trouser pocket which is housing my OS Explorer map (161 South London).

I've already rejected two lunch-stop benches as unsuitable; the first is surrounded by swampy grass, and the other is too low and too weird, with rough-hewn planks crawling with realistic carvings of giant insects. So, when I pass a 'just right' bench along a short stretch of the Crane, I gratefully sit down. The only problem is this tiny patch of riverside path is sandwiched between two very busy roads. I have the A312 Causeway in my left ear and the A30 Great West Road in my right.

Approaching Cranford, the route follows a generously wide tract of grassland before the path turns away from the river into residential streets. Every few minutes, a mighty roar heralded the appearance of the massive bulk of an airliner. A menacing shadow engulfing the houses in its wake. Flying so low, it was almost possible to read the maker's name on the landing gear tyres.

The river is re-joined a little further along the high street, and a pleasant walk through woods and parkland leads to a tunnel under the M4 motorway. A bit further, and the Hayes Bypass is negotiated. An iron bridge twists down to the Grand Union Canal and a mile along the towpath brings me to Hayes and Harlington Station and the first of three trains home.

Hayes to Moor Park: 7 December 2022 (18 miles)

I was able to catch a bus to today's starting point. The same bus could have taken me to Heathrow Airport with its promise of far-off lands and places whose names I have never quite got the hang of pronouncing. But my destination is somewhat less exotic, a bridge over a canal. To be precise, it's Bridge 200 next to Hayes and Harlington Station, and it will lead me onto the Grand Union Canal. Walking along canals is not my favourite terrain, but it's ok. Just happy to be out adventuring.

However, there is some early respite as the route takes a detour to visit Stockley Park. First, the business estate, salubrious with its green lawns and elaborate water features. It hosts some prestigious company offices as well as football's controversial video assistant referee (VAR) system. Crossing the road to the adjoining golf course, I encounter the usual navigational nightmare. I'm looking for a bridge that rises high above a busy dual carriageway and takes me into Stockley Country Park.

Given that the bridge's primary purpose is to give golfers access to a part of the course cut off by the road, I was surprised when a trio of golfers were less than unanimous when I asked for directions. 'Follow that path round to the right,' said one. 'No, best to go left and across the fairway,' said another. The third had nothing to add.

I resorted to dead reckoning by climbing the highest spots on this undulating course to spy the suspension bridge's tall concrete A-frame. On the other side, the path soon leads to a viewing point that looks south to the Surrey Hills. Then it's a descent through woods to rejoin the canal.

Another mile on the Grand Union before meeting the canal's Slough Arm, a five-mile dead end that peters out to a reed bed next to Shaggy Calf Lane, opposite is a pub that's been converted into a bathroom store. Honestly, with attractions like this, who needs to go abroad? I'm only doing the first mile, as far as the footbridge over the canal that will take me to meet the River Colne. Looking down on the towpath below, I recall that John Betjeman was quite rude about Slough in one of his poems. I wonder if he had ever walked along here and, if so, in which direction.

Soon I reach Little Britain Lake, so called because, from the air, it vaguely resembles the shape of mainland Britain, whether by accident or design, I do not know. I start just off Land's End, skirt northwards around Wales and the west coast of Scotland, leaving somewhere near the Outer Hebrides. A couple more miles follow the river, the first very enjoyable with a meandering path following the contours of the Colne through woodland. The second mile was less pleasant, reduced to a scraggy narrow strip of land sandwiched between the river and the boundary wall of the West London Industrial Park. It's almost a relief to be reunited with the canal.

I say almost a relief because it's a five-mile slog running north from Uxbridge. There is some welcome variation with an off-canal diversion via the adjacent Harefield Lakes. This is the first outing for my new boots, and I'm thankful to find a bench on a small roadside green to stop for lunch. Back on the canal for one last time to get to West Hyde, where I finally bid farewell to the Grand Union.

The trail climbs through woodlands and open farmland for five miles to reach Moor Park. Unexpectedly lovely countryside it is, so close to suburbia, but after 13 miles on flat ground, the hills are felt, and the stiles seem unnecessarily numerous and high. It's starting to get dark, but with a tricky section through the woods safely negotiated, it's just half a mile to the station along a path sandwiched between the railway tracks and Sandy Lodge Golf Club. Briefly, through the trees, I see a bright moon shining down on the deserted greens.

Moor Park to Stanmore: 14 December 2022 (10 miles)

Today's walk is on very familiar paths, which I have both walked and run for many years. This is the closest the LOOP gets to home, briefly visiting Hatch End and Harrow Weald before heading north.

I have always been astonished at this almost unbroken 10-mile tract of countryside on the edge of Greater London. And I've enjoyed it in all sorts of conditions; the mud bath of a New Year's Day, the scorching heat of midsummer, during the hope of early spring and the ambivalence of autumn. One of the most memorable times was getting caught in a hail storm wearing just running shorts and vest (it was early February, and I should have known better). But today trumps them all. Overnight snow has magically transformed my walk into a winter wonderland adventure.

The route starts by crossing Sandy Lodge Golf Club, its snowy-white blanket unbroken save for a few animal footprints, which I suspect were made by a fox. There is no need to heed the warnings of stray tee shots. It's likely to be a while before play will resume. It's a cold but clear sunny morning; the snow clouds that visited in the early hours have moved on. The ground slowly rises and, at the far end,

I'm rewarded by a view looking back down the course and across the Colne Valley beyond.

I buy coffee and a bun at a petrol station, then cross the busy main road to follow the LOOP sign into woodland that, in turn, leads to Oxhey Playing Fields.

It's not a sports field as you might expect, but an open space several hundred yards wide and over a mile long, gently undulating and interspersed with patches of woodland.

Leaving a narrow band of trees, the path stretches ahead, initially downhill, then climbing to an exposed bench on the edge of a small wood. An excellent spot to enjoy my coffee. A friendly dog wanders over to say hello and see if I have a piece of bun left. I return the greeting and explain I've already eaten the bun.

The route soon leaves this urban gem, veering off to the right to meet a road. But the countryside feel is quickly regained as we enter the northernmost section of Oxhey Woods. The next mile is an enchanting walk of snow-laden trees and winding paths until I get to Pinner Hill Farm.

Horses are stabled here, and the guidebook warns that the surrounding ground can be very muddy and should only be tackled if wearing wellington boots. It offers an alternative route, but as that's the one I usually take and never this one, I decline.

The cold weather saved me from the mud, but the hoof marks sunk deep into the ground have frozen into ankle-wrenching potholes. The LOOP sign points through the stable yard, but it feels wrong. Unable to find any other way, I tentatively proceed. Seeing a lady approaching one of the stable blocks, and to pre-empt a loaded 'Can I help you?' I ask for help first. She is friendly and tells me the route is in the other direction, a narrow path hidden behind a large piece of farm machinery. I mention the sign. 'Oh,' she says, 'one of the horses is a bit frisky and keeps knocking it with its head.'

After a half-mile road section, the LOOP follows close to the hedge line at the top edge of Grim's Dyke Golf Club and, once again, a great view beyond a desert of white.

Reaching Harrow Weald Common, the path twists between tall cedar trees and a series of wooden bridges that cross ditches and streams, adding even more magic to this delightful walk.

I am being spoilt today as the trail crosses another busy road into Bentley Priory Nature Reserve. A view, this time looking towards the City and Canary Wharf as the concrete path guides me towards Stanmore Common. The route winds around the frozen Stanmore Ponds, lakes really, with broken-off branches from the surrounding trees pointing skywards, trapped in the ice. Soon the LOOP is left for the day, and a link path takes me across the corner of Stanmore Country Park to the station. What an unexpected treat this has been.

Stanmore to Cockfosters: 30 December 2022 (18 miles)

Which year or town I forget, but I'm at work and on my own in the general office of a large supermarket. It's the early hours of the morning, and a software rebuild is slowly trundling to an end. Bored with how many revolutions I can achieve with one push of my swivel chair and frightened of the consequences further reading from my book might produce now that hot chocolate has replaced coffee from the canteen vending machine, my mind turns, not for the first time, to retirement.

Grabbing a piece of paper from the nearest printer, I sketch an idea that's been with me for a while. Could one walk around the edge of London, incorporating every Underground terminus along the way? I might write a book of my adventures, 'Beyond the End of the Line'. I mention this because today would probably have been chapter four.

Starting from the end of the Jubilee Line at Stanmore and passing the Northern Line's High Barnet terminus, the route heads east to Cockfosters, the enigmatic destination displayed on the front of eastbound Piccadilly Line trains. It means 'The Head Forester' or something.

It's a dismally wet day as I climb Stanmore Hill to rejoin the LOOP, and a potentially challenging one with many busy roads to negotiate. I head through the drizzle to Elstree, over the M1, and across the A41. A diversion around Aldenham Reservoir temporarily escapes a long section along a narrow pavement.

Many will remember Scratchwood as the first service station on the M1 going north, now renamed the rather grander London Gateway. Perhaps fewer know that an actual Scratch Wood gave it its name. It is sandwiched between the motorway and the equally busy A1 Barnet Bypass. But this short stretch of ancient forest is a delight and balm to road-weary feet. The entrance is guarded by an extravagantly tall wooden barrier. The guidebook suggests it might be to deter elephants. They may be right, as I don't see any.

The Barnet Bypass is heard before it is seen. The route continues on the far side of this six-lane highway, but to get to it requires a half-mile trek along a walkway uncomfortably close to the traffic to reach an underpass leading to a similar path coming back up the other side.

Cars can no longer access Moat Mount Open Space, but walkers can. It leads me to what promises to be one of the best parts of today's walk, following the Dollis Valley Greenwalk for four miles to High Barnet. But it's raining again, making it difficult to read my walking notes, which is the excuse I'm using for ignoring the instructions that direct me left to some steps down to a bridge and instead I carry on up the tree line path with stretches ahead up a steep hill. Realising my mistake when I reach the top, I employ faulty reasoning to correct it, resulting in an arduous two-mile road section and a boggy field passing as a nature reserve. Finally, I met up with Dollis Brook but missed the first mile, which is reckoned to be the best part. The rest is along a riverside path that is very muddy and sometimes flooded. Apparently, the route is best done in summer. I must come back.

The narrow footpath opens up to an expansive green space behind houses just before getting to High Barnet. Time for lunch, but Barnet Council has yet to see fit to install a single bench on this local recreational spot. Reaching a road, I find what looks to be a derelict sports ground. Probably shouldn't enter but can't resist a lonesome picnic table perched on a patch of grass. The table is not in mint condition, but I manage to balance on it somehow.

Post lunch, a stiff climb up Hadley Hill promises a view over London that doesn't materialise. However, an enjoyable walk into Cockfosters via Monken Hadley Common more than compensates. Reaching the outskirts of the town, I miss a turning and end up at a dead end on a housing estate. A gentleman catches up with me, says he thought I was lost, and gives me directions to the station. He looks and sounds like Martin Kemp, but I don't suppose it was.

Cockfosters to Chingford: 10 January 2023 (15 miles)

Before forming our hugely unsuccessful blues group, my friend Paul and I would spend much of the school holidays in one of three ways; listening to records while having endless Beatles v Stones debates, exploring local rivers, or exploring London with a Red Rover travel card. Over half a century later, I'm still following rivers, exploring London, and, yes, sometimes listen to the Beatles.

Today's start point is the Piccadilly Line terminus at Cockfosters which Paul and I must have visited, for the end of the line was always our objective. Even if it did shatter my earlier childhood belief that Golders Green, the last stop on the 183 bus, was a utopia of perpetual summer and no school.

After crossing Trent Country Park's extensive and wonderful countryside, the rest of the morning is spent following two rivers. The first is Salmon's Brook, meandering its way along the valley before the path climbs to Enfield Chase, the muddy riverside footpath promised by the guidebook, replaced by the broad and sandy Jubilee Path, although which Jubilee is unclear. A little further on, we join Turkey Brook, its fast-flowing caramel-coloured water rather un-brook like. The initial rural surroundings eventually give way to a much more urban one. But then it gets all country-fied again as the LOOP visits the Lea Valley and the south-west corner of Epping Forest. Sewardstone Marsh nature reserve, which provides a good, if chilly, lunch spot, is squeezed between the two.

The truth is, I've not been feeling all that well since mid-morning, and a post-lunch steep hill climb is approached with some trepidation. Several times I thought about finishing the walk early, and the possibility of a bus from the road at the bottom of the hill was considered. But then again, I could always turn back. It was quite a tough climb emerging on a barren hilltop, windswept by increasingly heavy rain. Still, at least there was a good view of the King George's and William Girling reservoirs.

The route skirts around the Scout Association HQ at Gilwell Park handy if I need some first aid. I'm close to Chingford now, but another challenge to face first. Following a path enclosed by trees, I almost miss the way marker that directs through a narrow gap leading to the top of an open hillside. There is no visible footpath, so I just head downhill and hope for the best. At the bottom I find a very muddy path that may or may not be correct. With only about half an hour's daylight left and feeling alone in the middle of nowhere, I cry out loud, 'You've got yourself into a bit of a fix again, haven't you?' No one heard. They weren't stupid enough to be out there. I am greatly relieved to find a LOOP sign, even if it does point up a muddy and slippery hill. I arrive safely, and thankfully, at Chingford Station in the rain and encroaching darkness to the welcome sight of a waiting train.

Chingford to Harold Wood: 25 January 2023 (17 miles)

A sunny clear day on a well-signed, easy-to-follow route across a fascinating part of rural Essex on dry and firm paths. Had I the patience to wait for spring, some of the above might have been true. Instead, I get poor signage on a path with as many twists and turns as a John le Carré spy novel, set in for the day mist, and, once released from its icy cage, mud eager to devour any unsuspecting boot.

The walk starts across Chingford Plain, which sounds more adventurous than it actually is. However, on this cold and icy morning, it has its challenges. After passing Queen Elizabeth's hunting lodge, another legacy of Henry VIII and his seemingly insatiable passion for 'sport', the LOOP heads east towards Chigwell.

There is a longer but more pleasant alternative route to the town. It avoids a tedious road section, favouring the Roding Valley Meadows Nature Reserve. Part of this was once RAF Chigwell, and there is plenty of evidence of its existence in the derelict concrete roadways and tethering blocks, for this base existed to build and launch barrage balloons during the war. As usual, I have the place to myself and can pause for a moment to wonder what ghosts lurk here. Imagining the bustle of everyday life as the day shift was coming on duty. At the same time, the night workers heading for a well-earned breakfast in the fug of the canteen. Maybe it wasn't quite like that, but it's how I imagine things.

At Hainault Forest Country Park, the route briefly joins a path around the lake before turning off to a large expanse of open grassland that climbs relentlessly towards the summit of Cabin Hill. Along with the guidebook and map, I've been using the excellent walking notes produced by the Inner London Ramblers. They have been invaluable throughout my LOOP adventures, so I can forgive the promise of a view towards Docklands, when the persistent mist produces a wall of impenetrable grey.

Reaching a band of trees that takes me across the golf course, those same notes accurately predict that there will be several fallen trees to negotiate along the path and that the yellow arrows on some of the surviving trees will be a better guide than the way markers.

Attempting such a long walk at this time of the year was always going to be challenging, and I'd realised I could only afford so many wrong paths. Careful navigation has mostly kept me out of trouble but used up time. When the possibility of a bus link from Havering-atte-Bower didn't work out, it left no choice but a final five miles cross-country with barely an hour and a half of daylight left.

From here, the LOOP shares the route with a local footpath, and the dual signage seemed good enough that I could save time by keeping the guidebook and map in my pocket. All ok until the waymarkers disappear after leading me towards some woodland. I think that there is bound to be a way out if I follow the path. But it goes around in a circle, returning me to my starting point. It's beginning to get quite gloomy now, and I'm wondering if this is one near miss or lucky escape too many.

Then through a gap in the trees and at the bottom of a steep slope, I spy a scrapyard, seemingly for large white vans. If there's a scrapyard, then there must be a road and a road that goes somewhere. Without even the faintest path to follow, I carefully make my way down. Perhaps not carefully enough, as I trip on some barbed wire hidden in the thick leaf mould, but I at least avoid colliding with a derelict Transit van. Made my exit, as nonchalantly as possible, towards the road I had felt sure must be there. Another lucky escape. The next and final LOOP outing comes with a tidal warning. I'll be fine.

Harold Wood to Purfleet: 19 April 2023 (14.5 miles)

After leaving Harold Wood Station, the first LOOP marker was a slightly faded small metal sign on a post pointing down a residential road. Unremarkable, you might think, but for me, it was a poignant moment.

I had planned to do this final section of the London LOOP on 8 February, but three days before, on a reasonably innocuous Sunday afternoon walk, I experienced a problem with my heart that required emergency treatment and a 10-day stay in the cardiac ward of our local hospital. A change of medication and a place on the waiting list for an ablation procedure has left me in limbo. Still, I thought I could manage this mostly flat and easy route. It does have refuge points where I could end the walk early if necessary.

Water has been a constant theme on the LOOP and continued with today's Tale of Two Rivers. The first is the Ingrebourne, met half a mile from the station, its source about 20 miles north at Brentford. It has welcomed a few tributaries on the way and is now set for its final few miles to meet the Thames. The LOOP joins it for the remainder of that journey. On the way, it will skirt the edge of the Pages Wood, not a wood but a forest sitting on the edge of suburbia, then across the marshland of the Ingrebourne Valley. Marshland might provoke images of Holmes and Watson battling through the fog on Dartmoor in *The Hound of the Baskervilles*. It's actually an easy-access concrete path with a large visitor's centre halfway along.

A brief visit to Rainham town centre (including the largest branch of Tesco one could ever hope to find). Then the final lap before the river turns left, as do we, to join the mighty Thames, now half a mile wide, on its eastward quest to the North Sea.

I took the alternative and arguably more pleasant path for this last section of the Ingrebourne. One that cuts across Rainham Marshes to meet the Thames just past the giant Tilda rice factory. Along the way are a couple of ornately stencilled fingerposts, not directing to the Thames as you might think, but to 'The Concrete Barges'. Built for the D-Day landings, they found a temporary role after the war to help with tidal defences before being towed to their final resting point and allowed to slowly sink into the Thames mud. A good and thoughtful place to stop for lunch.

Ten miles or so upstream, I could have been enjoying a walk on Bazalgette's Embankment or taking a cultural stroll along the Southbank. Here it's wilder stuff as the last few miles of the LOOP hug the northern shore of the Thames Estuary. The river is just a few paces to the right, and Rainham Marshes stretches away to the left. There is a strong headwind that impedes progress and, unfortunately, brings the pungent aroma of the upwind Rainham Landfill Site. The unappealingly named Coldharbour Point is passed, which becomes cut off if high tide reaches eight metres. Luckily today, it's only six.

The LOOP comes to a rather abrupt end when a signpost takes you away from the riverside path and through a short alley to a road with a pub on the corner, and that's it. The scaffold encasing the building gave the impression that it was closed. I later learned it wasn't and that I'd missed the opportunity of a celebratory pint. Instead, I made the short walk to the train station and home.

Usually, a circular route provides the satisfaction of returning to the start point. But having missed the ferry by nearly 170 years and under doctor's orders not to swim, the only option is to stare wistfully across the shimmering waters to the starting point, amongst the scrapyards of Erith. It's been an adventure, as always.

Chapter Two

The North Downs Way

My first long-distance path started on that wet November day, but the prelude was on a similar one six months earlier. Not on the North Downs, but the South. A good friend and I shared an ambition to do a long walk, something that could be done in a day but would be at least a marathon distance. When the opportunity arose to do a 45-kilometre (28-mile) charity walk, we signed up with alacrity. Not only would it fulfil that walking dream, but would also give us the opportunity to raise money for a local charity that works with young people caught up in gang culture, and on the beautiful South Downs.

That day had started overcast and turned to persistent rain by early afternoon. It made the steep ascents of the sometimes slippery and badly worn chalk paths especially challenging. The climbs would inevitably lead to a wind and rain-swept ridge stretching away into the distance. We kept ourselves going by taking advantage of the soup and chocolate bars offered at the refreshment points and by singing half-remembered Beatles lyrics.

Most of my walks up to that point had been in the part of the Chiltern Hills nearest to where I live, around Amersham, Chesham, and Wendover. Lovely though those parts are, and privileged am I to be able to access them, my South Downs adventure gave me a broader view of what might be possible with my weekly wanders.

The North Downs Way is a National Trail (17 at the time of writing) that follows the chalk ridge running from Farnham in Surrey to Dover in Kent. The distance is usually given as 153 miles, but that includes both alternative endings approaching Dover. Otherwise, depending on the chosen option, it would be 25 or 30 miles shorter. More of that later. I hadn't thought beyond the first stage as I set out.

Farnham to Guildford: 7 November 2018 (13 miles)

It was raining when I looked out the window at 6.30 am. Just as the BBC had predicted. Not the heavy downpour that will soon get bored and move on to annoy someone else, nor the light drizzle that can safely be ignored. But the set-in-for-the-day, wet-playtime sort when yellowing comics and old editions of the Blue Peter Annual, with the puzzles already filled in, are piled high on the teacher's desk. Thought of delaying my trip, but then asked myself, WWSSD? (What Would Scott or Shackleton Do?) Decided they'd have just carried on. And after all, we're talking about a few miles of tame Surrey countryside – not 600 miles across the Beardmore Glacier.

Waterloo Station was bewildering. Its 70 platforms (I may exaggerate) and the banks of departure screens made me giddy. South Western Railway was apologising for 'unavoidable delays' as I searched the displays for my train. Just as I thought I'd found it, the details would flicker and disappear, maybe reappearing briefly a couple of screens to the left or perhaps to the right – one could never tell. Eventually boarded the delayed and virtually empty 9.24 to Alton.

With suburbia left behind and the rows of houses and factory estates giving way to a more rural landscape, the rain stopped. I was encouraged when I saw a ray of sunshine falling on the corner of a distant field. But, stepping onto the platform at the unmanned Farnham Station, light rain had returned. Turn right up to the main road, right again, and there is the impressive metal art installation that marks the start of the National Trail. 'Dover 153 miles' it pronounced, and a small arrow pointed up the A31. Not for long, though, as the path soon dipped between hedges to join a quiet lane that followed the northern source of the River Wey. The adventure had begun.

Within a few hundred yards, the rain became heavy. My ill-fitting hood kept me dry but stopped me from seeing more than a few yards ahead; the only solution was alternating between keeping dry and hood removal to perform navigational corrections. A missed path early on (still raining heavily) caused a miserable 25 minutes when my new OS Explorer map was all but destroyed. It took a half-mile alleyway behind some posh houses to reunite me with the path.

The rain eased, and the trail was easily followed, even with a soggy map. It made its way east via roads, field paths, woodland tracks, and the inevitable golf course. Emerging from one of the woods into a large field, I spotted an orange football abandoned by the side of the path. Instinctively I moved toward it to kick a little further along the track. Just before doing so, I realised it wasn't a football but a pumpkin, and it wasn't alone. Several more lay scattered nearby. Well, only a week since Halloween. Perhaps someone's dumped them here, I thought. Then, more charitably, they've been left for the wildlife to peck and nibble at. Thought wrong again. A little further into the field, pumpkins stretched as far as the eye could see. They had to come from somewhere, and this looked like that place.

Having stopped for lunch in a bus shelter at Puttenham, the clouds lifted, and modest sunshine appeared. This was the best part of the day as the path climbed the Hog's Back, the western extremity of the chalk ridge that forms the North Downs, and perhaps my first taste of what's to come. The trail offered excellent views over the Surrey countryside before descending into woodland, where sunken paths threaded through a delightful autumnal landscape.

I left the North Downs Way, where it crosses the grandly named River Wey Navigation. Taking the riverside path north for a mile into Guildford. The city does not seem proud of its station and keeps it well hidden. The only clue was a small enigmatic sign on a lamppost stating 'Station 3 minutes' but without indication in which direction. Asking someone for help, I was told, 'Turn right and follow the road to the end, then go down the alley between the shops, over the canal footbridge, cross the road, and the station is on the right behind a high wall.' So it was, but even then, it gave little clue to its purpose.

I Caught the 3.45 slow train to London, which, due to continuing delays on a bad day for South Western Railway, was promoted to a fast non-stopper, but was actually a very slow non-stopper, to Waterloo. It crawled past each of the many stations it would generally have visited with the automatic announcement still reporting, 'The next station is Winthrop Green South' (or whatever), before warning of the gap between train and platform, quickly followed by 'Welcome aboard this South Western Trains service to Waterloo, stopping at... '.

I am glad to have started my first long-distance trail and overcome the weather and travel difficulties. Looking forward to the next section and whatever surprises it may hold.

Guildford to Dorking: 21 November 2018 (15 miles)

A few more miles than stage one and 20 minutes less daylight called for an early start. Still dark when I left home, but with no sign of the snowfall that some were predicting, so it was definitely adventure on. Plan was to get to Guildford by 10.00. However, a combination of overestimating the journey time and good fortune with train connections got me there just before 9.00. Coffee and bun bought from a stall on the station platform, and I was on my way.

Guildford and I didn't get on well when we last met. Still, with the help of Google Maps, I have been working on our relationship and was able to find the River Wey Navigation easily enough and follow its path a mile south to rejoin the North Downs Way. Early morning mist still played on the water's surface and the fields beyond.

I had been greatly anticipating the moment of setting foot on the trail again, and as I spied my first NDW waymarker of the day, fear I may have emitted an all too audible whoop of joy, possibly frightening a nearby dog walker and her dog. Yet, with all the stuff that clutters our minds and threatens our well-being, this simple act of putting one foot in front of the other, propelling us through delightful landscapes, is so liberating. I am always thankful for the opportunity to do so. Enough of the sentimental stuff – on with the story.

A mile across open land before the path starts to climb through woodland to a hilltop and St Martha's Church. Much of the North Downs is chalk, but here it is heavy sand and a bit of a toil on the long climb. The church's setting is stunning, with a panoramic view to the south. The mist was gone, replaced by a fine, clear day. I took the slight diversion to visit St Martha's and, if it was open, thought I might briefly look inside. As I approached the door, I heard raised voices from within. I couldn't make out the words, but it was enough to make me change my mind and walk on.

Going downhill was tricky as the sand diverged into several sunken and deeply rutted paths. I was relieved to meet the narrow lane leading me to the next part of the walk. After crossing the lane, there was a sudden and dramatic change. The sand was gone, and the reappearance of chalk with a short but steep climb to an open ridge. The view looking south was, what descriptor shall we use? Superb, breathtaking, magnificent, and anything else the thesaurus might dream up. It was definitely 'eyes right' for the next half mile until reaching a viewing point at the far end of the downland. This was Newlands Corner. With its large pay-and-display car park, visitor centre, and one of the best views in Surrey, my newly acquired guidebook calls this spot a 'honeypot'.

We are now at around 600 feet and will stay more or less at this height for the rest of the day. The trail continues along wide, straight paths through woodland with the odd tantalising glimpse of the same fantastic view through the trees. Along the way are several World War Two 'Pillbox' defences and a section called The Canadian Road, where their countrymen trained for D-Day. The path often opens up to short areas of heathland and unimpeded views. The NDW takes a sharp and unexpected right turn for the unwary (me), which leads to Blatchford Down and the perfect lunch spot.

Delightful woodland paths occupy the afternoon until a few miles outside Dorking, when the trail begins to descend into the town. Just before doing so, the oddly proportioned church of St Barnabas is passed on Ranmore Common, sometimes called The Church of the North Downs (although I'm sure there are other contenders). A little further, and as the trail begins to drop into the town, the Denbies Wine Estate is passed; acres and acres of vines stretching down the south-facing slopes. Finally, rounding a bend, the bulk of Box Hill appears on the other side of the Mole Valley. This will be my starting point next time.

I had the company of a fellow walker for the last couple of miles. He joined the path from another direction, and as we seemed to be walking at a similar pace, we quickly fell into conversation. He must be a few years younger than me as he asks for advice about his newly acquired Freedom Pass (a much-appreciated provision by Transport for London).

We soon learn that we have the same heart problem and have been on a pilgrimage; he, an official one in Spain, me on a homemade one taking members of the church I attend 17 miles to St Albans. I tell him about the reflective miles we did when a mile would be walked in silence. He likes the idea. In turn, I learn that he is a doctor, now semi-retired. Having no family ties, he uses whatever spare time he can afford to offer his services for protracted periods in third-world countries. There are two stations in Dorking, and we're heading for different ones. As we shake hands, he says, 'I do this keeping fit and all that, so I can continue my work abroad.' Adding poignantly, 'Otherwise, what's the point in me being here?'

Dorking to Merstham: 20 December 2018 (10 miles)

The last time I set foot on Box Hill was at 11.30 on 11 August 1999. I can be that precise because it was the day of the solar eclipse that skimmed the south-west tip of Britain. Fortuitously, work was taking me to the south coast that day, but I only got as far as Dorking by the time of the event. Thought it was just my crazy idea to climb the hill and was somewhat surprised to find a scene reminiscent of *Close Encounters of the Third Kind*: scattered groups sitting on the grass, looking skyward expectantly. It did get pretty dark, but this was not far enough south, with only Cornwall and parts of south Devon experiencing totality. I carried on my way.

This is the starting point for stage three of my North Downs Way adventure and is the shortest section so far. But it's also the toughest, with three climbs of 700 feet or more. The weather was excellent, and I was excited about the day ahead.

First, the River Mole must be crossed. I had read this could be achieved via stepping stones and was looking forward to doing so. But the river was far too high and fast flowing today – the stones invisible beneath its muddy-brown waters. A short diversion took me to an alternative crossing on the somewhat confusingly named Stepping Stones Bridge.

Was it me, or was Box Hill steeper than my last visit? I stopped at the official viewing point, not quite at the top, but the best place to enjoy the sweeping vista below and a good excuse to take a breather. The descent was tricky, with steep and uneven tracks threading through the trees, exposed tree roots a constant hazard.

The path came to a T-junction to meet another track coming uphill from the right. I suspected the missing fingerpost would have shown the NDW turned left uphill, but I wasn't sure. While checking the map, a runner and his dog came up the hill. He confirmed what I feared, the uphill track was the way to go. He seemed happy to fall in with my fast walking pace, and we walked together for a bit.

I learned he was from Sydney and had travelled around Britain for four years in a mobile home. His work, whatever it was, allowed him to move about the country. He loved the English countryside and the right to roam on endless trails and open land, especially being allowed to let his dog off the lead. Apparently not always the case in Australia. He said various difficulties made him realise it was time to return home. As he turned off, running again, I said, 'Hope things work out for you.' With typical Aussie optimism, he shouted over his shoulder, 'It will. It always does.' Once more, I'd found a temporary walking buddy.

Stopped for lunch at the top of Colley Hill at 738 feet. A splendid view looking to distant hills in the south, although it was a bit chilly. No more than a hundred yards behind me was the M25. It could not be seen but could most definitely be heard. Much easier going after lunch except for the mud, which was spectacular. Deeply rutted, narrow, ascending paths warranting level 4B in my mud grading system (unavoidable and perilous). A brief visit to Reigate Fort, built in the 19th century against a French invasion that never came, then a gentle drop down into Merstham in the dubious company of another golf course and the day's last encounter with the M25.

Merstham to Oxted: 16 January 2019 (9.5 miles)

Merstham occupies an ideal spot amongst the Surrey Hills, it's an ancient town with a long history dating back to the medieval period. But in modern times, it has gained the dubious company of the M25/M23 motorway junction on its doorstep. The westbound slip from Gatwick skirting around the edge of town like a protective arm.

Pleased to have arrived at the station and be on my way, despite the general greyness and mizzle in the air. The walk starts on Quality Street but soon turns onto a footpath that leads to a bridge over the M25, the motorway traffic thundering below. A short distance further and the busy London to Brighton A22 must be negotiated. No bridge this time, just a small central refuge island to aid the crossing. A steep path climbs through the trees on the far side, and I'm puzzled and slightly concerned by a prominent hoarding advertising cut-price skiwear. Next, the trail meets a lesser road which crosses high above one, then a second railway line.

Finally, a slightly unnerving tunnel under the M23 completes the tour of the local infrastructure. One of the only remnants of a more rural past is a medieval churchyard perched defiantly between the motorway and the trunk road. In fact, the sound of motorway traffic never ceased for the whole day, except for a very brief section when the A22 out-rumbled it.

Leaving the M23 behind, the route climbs diagonally up open ground, and it begins to feel like I'm on the trail. Near the top of the hill, the path narrows between hedges, and just as I reach this point, I'm nearly mown down by two galloping horses and their riders. Only had a few seconds to respond to the shouted warning and take evasive action, the traffic noise having masked their approach. Hoped they were nothing to do with the Apocalypse. I didn't note the colour of the horses.

Once recovered, I carried on to the trig point at the summit and took a breather and what I thought was a rather arty picture of a barren tree against the grey sky. Up ahead a large walking group blocked the now narrow path. They were huddled around their leader while he conveyed something of importance to them. They looked about my age and wore similar clothing (blue and red jackets in predominance). I felt strangely self-conscience as I threaded through their number, and, if I'm honest, a little grateful for my independence.

The rest of the morning combined woodland paths, roads, and hillside tracks. One of the paths led to open ground at the top of Gravelly Hill, the highest point of the day at 801 feet. A good spot for lunch. Found a wet bench with what would be a great view on a clear day but could only see the ubiquitous M25, all else lost in the mist. When I saw that same mist rolling up the side of the hill, I decided it was time to move on.

The afternoon was similar mixed terrain, but with the addition of several narrow, slippery chalk paths that I found hard to negotiate

THE NORTH DOWNS WAY

or even stay upright on. Maybe I should have bought some ski poles when I had the chance, but perhaps not the red salopettes. Later, the route turned sharply downhill to a mile north of Oxted, where this section ends. A mile to the station via another tunnel, this time under the M25.

In his wonderfully erudite book *London Orbital*, Ian Sinclair talks about walking within the M25's acoustic footprint. Undoubtedly true today.

It was still an excellent high-level walk, along woodland paths and open hilltops, if one could be inured to the traffic noise. Also, it leads to the more promising stage of Oxted to Otford, which includes the Surrey–Kent border crossing and the Greenwich Meridian. Exciting times are ahead.

Oxted to Otford: 23 January 2019 (14 miles)

Back to the Surrey Hills today for the next stage of the North Downs Way. Arrived at Oxted Station at 9.00 am, which is good going. Quick coffee, then a mile or so trek north to meet the trail. It's a cold day with snow lying on the higher ground but also bright and sunny, as these days so often are. I'd like you to share the journey with me as the NDW turns east for the 12 miles to Otford.

We are following the top edge of a large field that looks across the valley towards the southern hills. Such a great view that I almost miss the plaque that marks the crossing of the Greenwich Meridian. Through into a smaller field, then turning left onto a sunken track for the rather brutal climb to Botley Hill. Although this is the highest point along the entire North Downs Way at 853 feet, it disappoints, just a busy road junction. But we are soon rewarded with a fantastic open hillside climb with a diagonal path carving through the snowy grass. This is such a magical place with the view across the valley, the snow, and the refreshing breeze that it's tempting to linger. Still, there's no hurry and time enough to take a few photos and enjoy the moment.

Now the path dives through trees to meet a quiet road which, after half a mile, turns right into an even quieter one. This soon becomes a gravel track at the boundary between Surrey and Kent. Look, there's an NDW milestone to mark the occasion. After crossing a busy road, the trail enters a large field with views stretching into the distance. Turn uphill, then through a woodland path, still climbing, until we emerge again to regain the views. Enjoy this for a while until it becomes hidden by trees and hedges.

The next few miles are rather bleak, with large barren fields and difficult underfoot conditions. Eight miles completed, and time to think about lunch. But despite finding a gap in the hedge that briefly restores the view, there is nowhere to sit. Carry on for another 10 minutes when a minor navigational error brings us to a small village green with a large tree and two wooden benches, one of which is serviceable once the snow has been swept off. Don't want to stop here for too long as the weather appears to be closing in, and still several miles to go.

Back on the correct route and through an enchanting snowy wood that calls for more photos. This leads to yet more large and snow-covered fields. The views are hidden again, but it doesn't seem as bleak as the pre-lunch section. The path is good, the weather has relented a little, and a weak sun is doing its best to brighten the landscape. Not too much further, and we reach the top of Star Hill. Look down into the Derwent Valley and the grazing sheep on its slopes, a strong contender for 'View of the day'.

The path winds around the hill's contours until several signs advise taking an alternative, safer route, although safer from what it doesn't say. Take this reluctantly, as it means going uphill for a few hundred yards. Soon, though, we turn downhill to meet the road – an unpleasantly busy one adjacent to the M25. A bridge over the motorway leads to a few more roads and the final footpath of the day. This half-mile path crosses a couple of fields before climbing to join Otford High Street and, ultimately, the station. A challenging day but full of interest, with each new revelation inviting pause to appreciate.

Otford to Caxton: 26 February 2019 (16 miles)

This is the first section solely in Kent, plus it marks the halfway point of my North Downs Way project, so I'm very excited about the day. Up early to catch the 7.55 from Victoria, arriving at Otford for 8.30, a quick coffee and a bun at the station, then on my way.

The NDW is joined as soon as you reach the top of the station steps, so immediately on the trail. No chance for a gentle start, though, as soon the route goes off-road and up the steep climb to Otford Mount. There are a few more climbs throughout the day; some are rewarded with a beautiful view, as in this initial ascent, and others not, such as the stiff climb up Holly Hill later on. Unfortunately, there was also a somewhat hazardous descent which my ankle, damaged on a run 35 years ago, did not appreciate.

Generally, the going is easy with good paths alternating between woodland and open country, and all a sheer delight. Several miles follow the Pilgrims Way (no apostrophe needed). Although you might want to think you are following in the footsteps of centuries of penitents, the name was more likely to have been invented by an employee of the Ordnance Survey in the 19th century, while mapping these ancient tracks. One road sign says, 'PILGRIMS WAY LEADING TO BATTLEFIELDS'. I wonder if that is the sort of pilgrimage I really want to go on?

The sky has an exceptional quality today – deep blue at the top gradually fading to almost white at the horizon. A perfect backdrop for taking pictures of winter trees, which I did. As usual, not many people, but there was plenty of livestock. This included a small family of Shire horses, who looked at me quizzically, and an abundance of sheep, who looked at me sheepishly. 'Sheepish' also describes the first signs of spring, tentatively rising above the parapet of winter (sorry, I seem to have got a bit carried away here). Some early buds amongst the hedgerows and blossom on a few trees and a little more warmth in the sunshine. All are very welcome.

The M25 has been an unwelcome guest on previous outings, but today it was the M20 that ran close to the route. However, there has also been the quieter presence of the Greensand Ridge running parallel to the NDW and often visible a few miles south across the valley. This I do like, and now learning there is a Greensand Way, I'm eager to explore. But I mustn't be greedy, one trail at a time.

The last few miles are pretty remote as I penetrate further into the Kent countryside. It is also wonderfully peaceful. I can only think of one word to describe my enjoyment of today's outing, which may be a little out of fashion. Nevertheless, here it is… SPLENDID.

Cuxton to Bearsted: 13 March 2019 (15 miles)

It's a pleasant enough start to the day as the route crosses the expansive Ranscombe Farm Reserve, even if an early climb is a little taxing on travel-weary legs. But soon the path descends to the Medway Bridge which the North Downs Way shares with the M2 motorway, albeit unequally. The footpath is reduced to a narrow strip of tarmac which also serves as an emergency access lane, should the need arise. The fenced-off motorway is just a few feet to the right and to the left are the bridge railings. The river Medway can be seen, flowing 116 feet below. Today, the tide is out and a few small motor launches lie stranded on the sandbanks.

The bridge is over half a mile long and it's a relief when the path veers onto open land. It's a stiff climb but with good views back across the valley. I should describe the now receding motorway as a blot on the landscape, but I confess to finding its graceful curve quite elegant. The route follows a track through trees, then a minor road. A fairly tedious section with a steady climb but not rewarded with any views. After a couple of miles, though, a path appears to the right, which soon leads to the beauty spot Bluebell Hill and a stunning view to the south, unimpeded by any motorways, elegant or not.

Regular service is resumed as the trail drops to meet the A229 trunk road. The guidebook warns me to take great care along this next stretch – I do. I'm happy when the path turns away from the road to rejoin the Pilgrims Way, but my joy is short-lived. Wooden steps leading uphill are seldom a good sign, and these are no exception. A seemingly impossibly steep climb, twisting through a band of trees, provides an unwelcome pre-lunch challenge.

With a bit still to do before the path levels off to open ground, there's an NDW milestone. It tells me I've walked 79 miles from Farnham and it's another 46 to Dover (via the Folkstone route one presumes). I know this because I study the inscription longer than was entirely necessary, fooling myself it has sufficient significance to break my don't-stop-till-the-top rule. The climb has taken me back onto the chalk ridge that identifies the North Downs. A fallen tree trunk of suitable height provides a good if not perfect, place to stop.

After lunch, the trail begins to run south-east, which is good, but through the centre of a strange motorway-bounded acoustic corridor, which is not. The sound of the M2 in my left ear and the M20 in the right. Possibly the inspiration for Kraftwerk's *Autobahn*? I'll dig that out when I get home. But then again, maybe not. The path soon enters a wooded area that continues for most of the remaining four miles, still on the Pilgrims Way. Making a decent pace and feeling good.

I pass three runners doing their warm ups (which seems to include trying to push over a tree). A mile further on, and they overtake me. A further mile, just after the path turns right and goes sharply downhill, I meet them again, coming back up. This is getting a bit embarrassing, and I say something inane like, 'I used to do some of that and know how it feels, ha-ha.' Regret this as soon as they've gone by. A gentle drop into Detling, where this section ends, and a two-mile trek across fields to get to Bearsted Station and home. All in all, a much better day than I'd hoped for.

Bearsted to Charing: 26 March 2019 (16 miles)

The village of Woodstock is about nine miles west of my starting point today. This has reminded me it's 50 years since the festival of the same name. That fact and the seasonal change may be responsible for my somewhat reflective frame of mind. Recalling those poignant days, and perhaps the questioning lyrics of Joni Mitchell's 'Woodstock'. However, I better leave the existential musings until later as I need to catch the 7.55 from Victoria once again. This achieved, I arrived at Bearsted just after 9.00 am for the 30-minute walk back to Detling to pick up the North Downs Way from last time.

The trail soon begins the 500 foot climb up to the chalk ridge, which, once attained, provides uninterrupted and stunning views. It's a view you can never tire of, as each twist or turn in the path brings a new element to the vista while a previous one is lost. This even trumps an earlier stage, which I called 'Splendid'. Can't use that again, delightful seems woefully inadequate, and I can't find anything in the thesaurus that appeals, so I'll just have to make up a new word Triabluant? Lumbracous? Maybe not. Astonishingly, for the first eight miles of the walk, I see no living soul, not even a dog walker (no offence intended).

For the second half of the day, the trail rejoins the Pilgrims Way as it journeys relentlessly eastward via a combination of quiet lanes, tracks, and footpaths. Still an enjoyable experience, and again, barely another individual met. Unable to find a good place to stop for lunch, I settled for an uncomfortable log a few yards into the trees that run beside the path. But, as so often happens, a mile further and an ideal spot was passed: a picnic table, spring flowers, and a bench where, at one end, sat a monk. Well, a life-size wooden one, anyway. Head propped against his hand, contemplating or asleep it was hard to tell.

My guidebook finishes this section after 11 miles, having warned at the outset that this relatively short stretch, with its challenging climbs, should not be underestimated. However, I was still feeling good, so I continued for another five miles to Charing. On the way, I took a short diversion to see the Lenham Chalk Cliff, no rival for the White Cliffs of Dover but definitely worth a look. Climbing back up the steep side of the gully I'd descended to get a better view, a group of ovine onlookers surround the edge. They look about as threatening as sheep can get, which isn't very much.

I have felt more 'in the country' here than on any other section so far, and it has definitely been a triabluant day, quite lumbracous in fact (I hope that's not something rude in another language).

Charing to Sandling: 3 April 2019 (20 miles)

Up at 5.30 am to an unpromising prospect. Hadn't slept well, developed a rather unpleasant head cold, dubious weather forecast, and planning by far the longest and most challenging walk of this project. In the days when I would go for an early morning run, these are the circumstances I would be told that I was foolish to go and obsessed with running. But I would go anyway and probably develop a chest infection a few days later.

Common sense would decree that I shouldn't go, so I did. Arrived at Charing at 9.20 am in need of coffee, but oddly, the village café didn't open until 10.00 am. Next best, try the local grocery store as they often have a coffee machine. No luck there. I was advised to go across the road to the butchers who boiled a kettle and produced a cup of the instant stuff in a plastic cup. Oh well, it would have to do.

A gentle start on a level and good path continues along the Pilgrims Way before cutting across broad open fields. A significant point along this section occurs at Boughton Lees, where the North Downs Way offers a choice of routes: a northern one via Canterbury or a southern option via Folkestone, both heading for Dover. I was taking the generally preferred southern path (I may return to do the northern route one day). The guidebook has warned me it will be a challenging walk, but not without its rewards.

The first town after the paths split is Wye. The sun is shining, and trees that line the road display an abundance of showy blossom. Spring has arrived. The trail soon climbs steeply to Wye Crown, where a fabulous view awaits that my camera cannot do justice to. Had my lunch here, but typical of the fickleness of the season, it's pretty cold, and the threat of rain hangs in the air. I hurried on.

It's half a mile along the top of the chalk ridge until the view is temporarily lost, but the route remains high level as it switches between quiet lanes, bridleways, and paths. There is still a sense of altitude along this near-deserted trail. Some miles later, the arduous climb up Cobb's Hill restores the splendid view, only this time there is the timid appearance of the sea on the far edge of the horizon. An exciting section now with deep grassy gullies and ridge-hugging narrow paths across Postling Downs before the day's final climb up to the Tolsford Hill Radio Station. This is now used as a mobile phone mast and for DAB radio transmission. In its glory days, it carried the Eurovision Link across to the continent, including, one presumes, the song contest in its milder days.

A less bashful seascape now becomes centre stage, with the sweep of the bay curving into the distance. I must say goodbye to the NDW here to transfer to the Saxon Shore Way to get to Sandling Station. I had booked a specific train to get a cheap fare on HS1 and thought I had plenty of time. But the path proved more difficult than expected, producing a fraught last mile with some brisk walking and a bit of running. Made it with minutes to spare. Just the final leg to Dover next time – where I must remember to stop.

Sandling to Dover: 10 April 2019 (15 miles)

The *Official National Trail Guide* is very enthusiastic about this final section of the walk, promising spectacular views and much to interest the walker. Whether or not it lives up to this, we'll see later. But first, I must face the two-mile slog on a crumbling path back up Tolsford Hill to meet the North Downs Way for the last time. This achieved, the narrow path runs between a grove of hawthorn trees which was preceded by a warning sign that the area is used for army training and not to stray from the footpath. I don't.

With that behind, it's a long climb up a steep combe which is rewarded by a fine view looking west. A lone diminutive tree clings tenaciously to the windswept edge of a path that hugs the contour of the hillside. The route now makes a purposeful left turn up a flight of wide grassy steps that set the easterly direction that will prevail for most of the remaining part of the day. Now with the sea to my right and the enormous Channel Tunnel terminal directly below. This will be replaced by vertiginous chalk cliffs later on.

Crossing a minor road, I make way for someone coming over the stile that will take me into the next field. It's a steep bank down to the road, so I wait patiently at the bottom. Then someone else appears, and then another. Finally, after about the sixth walker, someone takes pity on me, suggesting I get over quickly as many people are behind. There were about 40, probably more people than I'd met on the last three sections of the walk put together, and a reminder that things might get a bit busier than I'm used to.

The top of Dover Hill is reached, and an opportunity to stop for lunch. But I can only find a low stone slab to sit on next to the trig point. There is such a strong offshore wind that the only way I can stop my rucksack from blowing down the hill towards the sea is to jam it under my right leg. It's cold here, and I don't linger. A little further, I reach The Battle of Britain Memorial with its two spitfires on show outside the main building. They may only be replicas but are poignant enough to provoke an emotional response at the thought of those young men, some still in their teens, taking to the skies in the real things.

Now I meet those white cliffs and the high-level path that will take me another four miles almost to Dover. With its dramatic seascape, this should be exhilarating and enjoyable, but I am now fighting a relentless headwind. The path is prodigiously undulating with little level ground; the sea, a long way below, appearing for a while, then hidden from

36

view until the next hilltop or bend. But I still appreciate the walk, although it seems to take an awfully long time to get to the town.

Approaching Dover, the NDW does a nasty thing: it leaves its easterly progress and turns inland to curl around the back of the town, adding a couple of unnecessary hills. Eventually, I arrive at the seafront and literally the finishing line, which I initially miss, expecting something vertical. But there it is, an eight-metre metal finish/start line embedded in the paving. When I spot it, I think, 'Oh good, that's done.'

Did the day live up to expectations? Perhaps not quite. Yes, the countryside and sea views were grand, and I have left much out here for the sake of brevity, but it was a bit too busy and noisy, and I preferred the remote, tranquil sections of some of the previous stages. As this will be my last North Downs Way report, I hope you will indulge me with a few more lines for concluding thoughts.

This is the first long-distance path I have completed, albeit over a protracted period, and it has been a wonderfully enjoyable and satisfying venture. I have loved the novelty of each section, not knowing what the day has in store or even what's around the next bend. I feel fitter, thanks to all those challenging climbs, and a bit wiser if you will allow the pretension. It could be one or two people I met on the way, the places visited, or all the thinking done. Maybe the beginning of wisdom is discovering how much you don't know or understand?

Another thing I don't know is where my wanderings will take me next. However, if I may misquote a geographically relevant musical reference, 'We'll meet again, don't know where do know when.' It will probably be a Wednesday.

The North Downs Way Alternative Ending
The Canterbury Trails

'The Wanderer's Story' (Pt1) Wye to Canterbury: 24 August 2022 (14 miles)

It's nearly four years since I started on the North Downs Way. It was my first long-distance path, and I remember it fondly. But there's an alternative ending which I should have gone back to do. At Broughton

Lees, 30 miles from the finish, the path splits to offer two routes to Dover. I'd taken the more favoured southern option via Folkstone. The original walk was done through autumn, winter, and spring, so completing the job by doing the northerly route, via Canterbury, in the summer felt appropriate.

The 7.37 HS1 from St Pancras whisked me to Ashford International in under 40 minutes. Time for coffee and a bun before taking a slower train to the town of Wye. From there, it was a couple of miles to get back to where the path splits. It was good to see those familiar NDW waymarkers again, a lot has happened since we last met.

Much of the way was across stubble-filled fields that shone a bright orangey-yellow and stretched to the horizon. Never content, it seemed, with flat ground but sweeping gracefully downhill, inevitably leading to a stiff climb on the other side. There were also acres of orchards, each with the temptation of ripe fruit asking to be picked. At one point, the route crossed what is apparently the largest orchard in the country, a mile and a half of immaculately spaced apple trees. But there were also woodland paths and sheltered green lanes, enjoyable enough in their own right but also bringing some welcome shade from the midday sun.

Inevitably, some of the route follows The Pilgrims Way, and there was an information board at a gap in the tree-lined path. It explained that from here the pilgrims could get their first glimpse of Canterbury Cathedral. I tried and tried, but I couldn't see it. Maybe I'm just not holy enough.

I've only visited this city once before and as that was for work there was no time for sightseeing or homage paying. It's been a hot day, the paths dry, and the hill climbs taxing. I got as far as the city gate and the road that would take me to the cathedral. But the thought of joining a tourist queue in my dusty and thirsty state didn't appeal; the flesh was weak, and I turned away to find a pub. At least I resisted a second pint, and I had arrived here on foot, which must count for something?

'The Wanderers Tale' (pt2) Canterbury to Dover: 31 August 2022 (21 miles)

Today's walk was the concluding part of the alternative North Downs Way ending. The trail guide divides this section into two stages, but I thought it could be uncomfortably done in one.

It took a couple of miles to exchange the city for the countryside, but it was not for the orchards, woodland paths, or rolling arable fields of Part 1. Now it's a much more open and sparse landscape. I'd read that the fields were large enough to hold several dozen football pitches, or considerably more tennis courts, using the comparisons often used for such purposes.

The path gradually climbs to the wonderfully named Womenswold. The names of other villages passed through are also worthy of mention: Patrixbourne, Shepherdswell, Coldred, and my favourite, Waldershare. It was at Shepherdswell that I stopped for lunch. It's been sunny but pretty windy, and I'm glad to find some shelter here. Struggled a bit post lunch with some tricky terrain, and being concerned about missing my Dover train, I increased the pace. For most of the last six miles, the path is narrow and enclosed as it joins up with the White Cliffs Country Trail, heading due south to the coast – only it didn't.

A mile from Dover, and having made up lost time well, the path was blocked by extensive earthworks. Diversion signs left me in the middle of a large, stubble-filled field. Cutting my losses, I headed for a road and navigated a route into town as fast as my 20 mile legs would allow. Made the train with 10 minutes to spare. Just enough time to buy an ice-cold Diet Coke, sink into my seat, and contemplate that my North Downs Way adventures have finally ended.

Chapter Three

The Ridgeway Path

Like the North Downs Way, The Ridgeway mainly follows a chalk ridge and is a National Trail but maybe a more prestigious one. A walk that is much written about and photographed. I had enjoyed the solitude of the North Downs and was worried this latest venture would be too busy, imagining queues crossing stiles matching the pictures one sees of the line of people waiting their turn to step onto the summit of Everest, minus the discarded oxygen bottles, of course. I needn't have worried.

The path runs north-east from its start at Overton Hill in Wiltshire, across South Oxfordshire, and eventually into North Buckinghamshire. It finishes at Ivinghoe Beacon. No actual beacon but a trig point, a Ridgeway map, and a splendid view across the Vale of Aylesbury.

Overton to Fox Hill: 3 May 2019 (18 miles)

I'm listening to *Rubber Soul*. Track after track from my favourite Beatles album filling the space inside my small car. With just a couple of songs to go, a pop is heard from the speakers and the music stops. I know I've been playing it too loud, and now it's broken. No amount of switching on and off or adjustment makes any difference. I continue in silence.

I'm heading for Fox Hill, a few miles south-east of Swindon. This will be my end point for today's first section of my new adventure. A bus into town and then another to Avebury will get me within a couple of miles of the Ridgeway's start at Overton Hill. A brief but fascinating visit to the Neolithic standing stones at Avebury (second only to Stonehenge and much more accessible). Then the two-mile walk to the start of the Ridgeway.

I'm well equipped for the trail with an OS map, the excellent A to Z route guide, and two guidebooks. Perhaps a bit of overkill as the route is so well marked with its distinctive rich brown fingerposts and inlaid white lettering – the first announcing 'Ivinghoe Beacon 87 Miles'. After an initial climb between hedges, the path reaches the top of the chalk ridge. It will stay at this high level for most of the day, getting to almost 900 feet at times. I have often admired the landscape from the M4 motorway, but standing in this expanse of open space, a gentle breeze and views stretching to the horizon in almost any direction one cares to turn, is a new and wonderfully intoxicating experience.

The views are briefly lost when the path drops into Ogbourne St George. Just as I'm about to join the path that climbs back up from the village, a man stops me. 'You're walking quite fast,' he says. 'What pace do you think you are doing?' I tell him what my watch tells me, an average speed of 3.7 mph. He seems impressed and tells me he has been researching walking pace, and my speed is above average. It seems an odd thing to say, but then I remember there was an article about just that in last week's *Sunday Times*. Maybe he wrote it. Who knows?

I had covered 18.5 miles by the time I got back to the car – the completion of a most enjoyable first day on the Ridgeway. I change my shoes, take a few gulps of water and settle into my seat for the drive home. Push the starter button, and the engine fires to life effortlessly. A few seconds later I'm startled as a loud noise hits my ears. But it's ok, in fact it's more than ok -The Beatles are back!

Fox Hills to Bury Down: 5 June 2019 (17 miles)

A lot has happened in the month since I was last in the Wiltshire village of Fox Hill. I went on holiday as planned, then spent three days in the cardiac ward of Corfu Hospital, which wasn't. It makes me all the more eager to return for the next stage of the Ridgeway Path. Taking the 8.15 from Paddington to Swindon, then to the somewhat uninviting bus station for the 25-minute journey to my starting point.

A kind friend has offered to pick me up at Bury Down in South Oxfordshire, where this section ends. This will save me a tiresome journey to the nearest station at Didcot following a long day.

His passion is for trains, and he will use the opportunity to take a return train trip on the recently electrified track between Newbury and Reading before collecting me. Each to his own.

I must admit to an almost child-like excitement setting out on the trail. I am thankful to continue this simple pleasure that has brought me so much enjoyment. A few hundred yards of steady climb and the features of stage one are regained: expansive panoramic views, birdsong, a gentle breeze, and the intermittent but pungent *'parfum de ferme'*.

At some point, I slip across the border between Wiltshire and Oxfordshire. The landscape becomes more subdued for a while, and I'm beginning to think I've left the best of the views behind. Then I reach the summit of Whitehorse Hill with the Vale of White Horse stretching north, seemingly to infinity.

But walking along, I begin to ponder, not for the first time, why we react as we do to our natural surroundings; is it some primordial remnant in our psyche or something we learn through experience? Still thinking it through, but I suspect a bit of both. After nine miles, it's time for lunch, sitting on a grassy bank, enjoying this fantastic view and fine weather.

The afternoon started with a bit of a plod along a three-mile section of chalk path with more restricted views. I'm a bit weary, although still keeping a good pace. I feel better when the trail turns north-east, and the landscape opens up again. Now following a broad grassy track that will take me the last four miles to Bury Down. My friend is waiting to collect me – waving from the Ridgeway notice board. A pleasant drive home ends a super day.

Hopefully, stage three in a couple of weeks, when we shall join the Thames for a bit.

Bury Down to Nuffield: 19 June 2019 (18 miles)

Once again, my kind railway enthusiast friend helps me out. I park my car at Nettlebed, the nearest point to today's finishing point at Nuffield, and he drives me back to Bury Down. On the way, I hear all about converted D-stock, the trains that used to run on the London Underground's District Line but have found a new lease of life on cross-country National Rail routes. Although I'm not especially into rolling stock, I find it fascinating, and I'm caught up with his knowledge and enthusiasm. I'm also told to look out for a bridge where the Ridgeway crosses a disused line. I do find it and oblige with a photograph.

This middle section of the Ridgeway links the wide, open spaces of Wiltshire and South Oxfordshire with the northern escarpment of the Chiltern Hills. It does so via a fairly long stretch along the River Thames, but more of that later. My starting point at Bury Down is in the middle of nowhere. Any inhabitants left the area around 3,000 years ago. Unfortunately, they took all the coffee shops with them, so I couldn't get my usual kick-start.

The first seven miles still have the open landscape of early sections; even when the path is enclosed by hedgerow, the view is always close and reappears in the gaps. But eventually, we descend into Goring to meet the river. Shortly before this, I am delayed by a dog walker who wants to discuss Brexit and international conspiracy theories. I listen patiently. Luckily the dog doesn't and provides the catalyst to set me free. Due to this delay and the coffee situation, I decided to take lunch earlier than usual. At least this means my soup is still nice and hot, silver linings and all that.

Now the six mile stretch along the Thames towards Wallingford. Much of this alternates between roads through pretty villages and paths alongside the river. Neither of these I find particularly inspiring, although, along with classical music, I feel I should. It is a relief when the trail turns sharp right, leaving the river and regaining an easterly direction. But soon, the footpath becomes narrow, twisting, and somewhat slippery, sometimes treacherously so. This is interspersed with easier woodland paths, much more like the Chiltern tracks I'm used to.

I hoped to complete the final four miles in time to catch the 16.10 bus back to my car in Nettlebed, but the tricky conditions meant I was 10 minutes late. However, as I approached the bus shelter, the X38 Connector came speeding to a stop. I made it with a combination of my running and an obliging driver. Had I been a few minutes earlier, I would have assumed I had missed it and set out on the unwelcome two-mile trek along the main road, and the bus would have flown by.

Another silver lining. A gently refreshing light rain for most of the afternoon but not the downpour reported from home – this time, not even a dark cloud to contain any lining.

Nuffield to Princes Risborough: 3 July 2019 (16 miles)

The walk starts at Nuffield in south Oxfordshire, initially across arable farmland on a well-defined path running downhill through the middle of a glorious carpet of three-foot-high wheat, then back up towards woods on the far side. After a couple of miles, the route sets its sights relentlessly north-east. A level path between hedgerows until the tunnel under the M40 motorway, then along chalky paths leading to Bledlow Ridge, tree-lined for much of the way.

It was a hot day, and the level, straight paths with little scenery to detain, induced me to walk faster than necessary and probably not drink enough water. Stopped for lunch perched on some old farm machinery abandoned at the side of the track. Not the most comfortable spot, but I needed a break. Another mile or so and the Ridgeway took a half-right turn to visit Lodge Hill, a steep climb in the heat but a good view across Princes Risborough and the Vale of Aylesbury beyond.

And Princes Risborough is where I should have stopped. Surely 15 miles on a hot day was enough? The station and a relaxing journey home beckoned, and maybe an ice-cold Pepsi. But I didn't. Thought I could do a few more miles to Great Kimble and get a bus back into town. All ok until faced with the steep steps that lead up the last stretch of Brush Hill. I sat on the bottommost step and finished what little water I had left and went to go, but couldn't. The heart arrhythmia that intermittently haunts me was manifesting itself. I sat down again and contemplated my predicament: I couldn't continue uphill or walk back to the station.

I was, and still am, incredibly grateful for the kindness of two passing strangers: Phil, who stayed with me as I made my way painfully slowly onwards carrying my rucksack for me as we went; and Anthea, who went home to collect her car, met us in the car park with a supply of biscuits and fresh water, then drove me to the station.

Two things I learned from the day: I'm not as indestructible as I once thought, and more importantly, there are still good people out there.

Princes Risborough to Wendover: 10 July 2019 (6 miles)

I did a short section of the Ridgeway today, just six miles from Princes Risborough to Wendover. The path traces the Chiltern Hills' northern escarpment, each new hilltop presenting a different view of the vast Vale of Aylesbury, stretching out to the north. These exposed hilltops are connected by twisting woodland paths and some flatter open ground.

After my slight difficulties at the end of the last section, my first objective was a trouble-free ascent of Brush Hill. Relieved to have achieved that, I stood by the trig point, admiring the view and having a little ponder. My thoughts were interrupted by an older couple coming from the other side of the hill. We chatted for a few minutes; I learned that she was going home for a Zoom art lesson and he to have a sleep. Somewhat randomly, the gentleman said, 'You don't have to believe everything in the Bible, but it does say you can live to 120 and that you should take a little wine for your stomach's sake.' Uncertain about achieving the suggested longevity but happy with the wine tip.

I feel uneasy when the path crosses the Chequers Estate with its multitude of cameras plotting my progress. But it's good to see that this country seat of power cannot resist the progress of a national path, and it does give me the chance to compose the first verse of a political protest song. I don't sing it aloud in case microphones are hidden in the grass. With its panoramic view, Coombe Hill is enjoyed before the Ridgeway descends into Wendover.

Only a few miles until I reach Ivinghoe Beacon and the trail's end, so what next? Thinking about the Icknield Way Path, which continues from Ivinghoe and eventually stops along the Suffolk–Norfolk border. Something to think about anyway.

Wendover to Tring (filling in the gaps)

I don't have a contemporary write-up for this penultimate section of the Ridgeway, but as it's a stretch I have done many times as part of other walks, I decided to do a brief route description. Just to complete the picture.

You used to be able to get coffee and a bun from a pleasantly rustic café on the platform at Wendover Station – rough wooden tables and an eclectic collection of chairs. It was also the only place I've found that still sold Fruit Polos. It is missed, but the trail continues through the town centre, which has a few other coffee options. A Ridgeway fingerpost points down an alley just before the parade of shops end and follows a small stream past an open space and a lake to a road opposite a grand-looking church. Turn left here and follow the road to a T-junction. Then it's straight across to follow a very narrow lane that gets increasingly steep and rugged until reaching a dead end by a farm building. A short track leads into the woods. The path turns left and uphill, climbing between the trees.

It's near here I once met a forest ranger who put me on the spot by asking me to guess how many acres of land were owned by the Forestry Commission in Britain. Tried to make a sensible guess but didn't want to deflate his moment by guessing too high or sound silly by going far too low. 'Two million acres?' I ventured. It was 50 million (phew!).

Woodland paths predominate for most of the walk, occasionally meeting with the Icknield Way. A short road section past Hastoe leads to the grand finale through Tring Park. Occasional gaps between the trees reveal stunning views which stretch immediately below your feet, into the middle distance, and away to the horizon. A highly photogenic scene. Tring station awaits at the far end. Like many country stations, it's a fair distance from the town. But we're not going there – the last few miles of the Ridgeway lie in the other direction and will be reported on in the first section of my next project – The Icknield Way Path.

Chapter Four

The Icknield Way Path

The Icknield Way is thought to be the oldest trail in the country. Predating the Romans, it ran from Dorset to the Norfolk coast. It was a ghostly presence when walking the Ridgeway Path, sometimes manifesting as a shared way, sometimes a cross-path. The Icknield Way Path has been created to keep as near as possible to those ancient tracks. It takes over where the Ridgeway finishes at Ivinghoe Beacon and runs for 108 miles across six counties to Knettishall Heath on the border between Suffolk and Norfolk. Generally, the signage just calls the route the Icknield Way, so I shall do the same or shorten it to IW. The last three miles of the Ridgeway Path are included in the first stage, as it was walked on the same day.

Tring to Dunstable: 24 July 2019 (17 miles)

This week's Wednesday Wander says goodbye to the Ridgeway Path and hello to the Icknield Way; completing the remaining few miles of the Ridgeway and covering the first 10 of the Icknield Way.

Oddly, I arrived at Tring Station a little ahead of schedule due to a delayed train. Mandatory bun and coffee before setting out for Ivinghoe Beacon. It's promising to be a very hot day, so I'm carrying enough water to fill a small reservoir. This last stretch of the Ridgeway takes an hour, initially climbing through woodland, then crossing wide open fields before the very steep path up to the Beacon and the end of my Ridgeway adventure. I enjoy the views and some of that water, take a few photos, then retrace my steps to find the start of my new challenge.

Finding the Icknield Way signpost, I head north-east across open ground to a cool and peaceful fir-tree wood a mile later. I've been here before on the Ashridge Boundary Trail, and I know that up ahead is a punishing 300-foot stepped climb, like climbing the stairs 20 times.

A remote hilltop farm is reached, but apart from a few bored looking sheep, it seems deserted of life, just old farm machinery and a few tyres. A long, hot, dusty, but thankfully downhill path to the village of Dagnall and another arduous uphill climb to Whipsnade Golf Club. I get lost here as I lose sight of the waymarkers. Still, a combination of the OS map and my emergency GPS device gets me sorted – well, physically sorted. The gizmo doesn't do existentialism, unfortunately.

The path now skirts around the edge of Whipsnade Zoo's perimeter fence before emerging at the road. A first in lunch-stop venues is the Whipsnade Tree Cathedral, created by Edmond Blyth in the 1930s as an act of 'Faith, hope and reconciliation' following his memories of World War One. I find a shady spot on a low stone bench in the Easter Chapel.

Not long after restarting, the route makes a sharp right turn onto the magnificent Dunstable Downs. The views equal or surpass any I've seen in the last few weeks. The impressive Chiltern Gateway Centre sits at the back of the hillside. It commands a fantastic view on this fine day as the Vale of Aylesbury spreads out like a giant green and gold patchwork quilt stretching to the horizon. Being so warm, I decided to stop for a cold drink. While queuing, I spotted a fridge filled with individual ice-cream tubs. The sort you could buy from the usherette in the cinema. Only they weren't. Picking one up, I was puzzled that they chose the illustration of a paw print on the lid. Then I read the label on the side... it was ice cream for dogs. Settled for a piece of fruit cake instead.

It's another three miles before the trail drops into Dunstable. I am reflecting on what a great day it's been and how I might convey this to you when navigational difficulties (not entirely of my own making, I like to think) land me on the carriageway of the A505 east–west trunk road. A harrowing 400 yard walk along the roadside gets me to the junction with the A5 and the relative safety of a narrow pavement. But I'm further north than I want to be, so a tiresome two mile walk back into town is required. Still, no major problems today, which is good going on recent form, and I really enjoyed the rapid transit link, half bus, half train, that takes me to Luton Station.

Dunstable to Luton: 16 August 2019 (18 miles)

However circuitous a route you chose, you'd be hard pressed to create an 18-mile walk between these neighbouring towns. But on a day fraught with difficulties, I managed it.

I hoped to get as far as Hitchin today, a distance The Icknield Way Association's *A Walkers' Guide* considers worthy of two days to complete; only I knew better, thinking I'd do them both in one.

Not a great start when the path takes a lengthy diversion around an extensive redevelopment area. The ancient Icknield Way ignominiously shepherded between temporary metal fence panels stretching downhill for half a mile. The path was barely passable in places as weeds and shrubs had been allowed to grow to almost the top of the six-foot-high fence. A little fooled by a bridge over a new bypass that was not shown on either the OS map or the route guide until, at last, some proper countryside was reached. But it was worth the wait, with beautiful vistas opening up to the north and east. Crossing Sundon Country Park, the hillside dropped to green pastures stretching below. A long line of sheep had congregated near the boundary fence at the top of the field. Almost as one, they turned to face me, resembling spectators along a marathon route urging the runners on. 'Come on, Mark,' they seemed to say, 'you can make it.'

From the highest point of the morning, the path made a spiral descent into the village of Streatley. The views from this helter-skelter of a path were superb. Stopped for lunch, sitting on a bench outside Streatley Church, where the guidebook ends this section. Despite the relatively short distance, I felt a little weary, and it had started raining. The sensible thing might have been to stroll across the road to the bus shelter and wait half an hour for a bus to Luton, but, unsurprisingly, I didn't. Instead, I set my sights on Hitchin.

All ok for around three miles, then it all went wrong. Coming to a cross-path, I searched for an Icknield Way sign. The only one I could spot was directing straight across, it seemed reasonable enough to follow this, but I had doubts. So much so that after several hundred yards, I returned to the junction to recheck. No, the sign was quite emphatic. Straight on was the way to go. After a mile, a signpost sends me sharp left, which I am unhappy about as it's due west, and I should be heading east. I hoped it would turn east, or at least north-east, further along. It didn't, and I realise I'm heading back to the A6 Luton to Bedford Road that I'd crossed an hour ago. It's clear I can't complete the walk, and I better call it a day and try to catch that Luton-bound bus.

I now see that I had picked up the Icknield Way Trail (rather than Path). This cycle and equestrian route runs parallel to, and sometimes shares, the walking route. I was following it back towards Streatley, where the paths had diverged. I waited an hour for a bus that didn't come, so I braved the steady rain and started to walk the four miles back into town. Of course, two minutes later, a number 79 raced past. My cries of 'No! No! No!' were lost in the wind, rain, and traffic noise.

From my working days, I remembered there was a service road leading to a branch of Homebase at the second roundabout. You never know, there might be a bus stop, a coffee machine, or even just a Mars Bar placed amongst the other entrapments at the checkout. Anything to bring me comfort. Ten minutes later, I returned to the road empty-handed.

On the outskirts of town, there was a petrol station where I could purchase some victuals. 'How's your day going?' the friendly cashier inquired. 'Great,' I lied. 'Really good.' He seemed unconvinced. Managed to get a bus for the last mile but hadn't bargained on it visiting every local housing estate along the way. It didn't matter, though. I was dry, not walking, and on my way home.

Luton to Baldock: 28 August 2019 (13 miles)

The first two stages of the Icknield Way had many twists, turns, and loops. Had it been built by the Romans, it might have suggested a homesick surveyor seeking solace in the company of Bacchus. However, today's route is pretty straight as it strikes north-east from Bedfordshire into northern Hertfordshire.

A train to Luton and a short bus ride get me a few miles north of the town centre and onto a footpath which, after a mile, will lead to the cross-track where it all went wrong last time. I spend some time searching around the junction that caused me so much trouble, and then I see it. A wooden post bearing an Icknield Way sign, half leaning into the bushes. I feel better about missing that in the rain, weariness of limb, and confusion over the alternative route sign. This spot, Maulden Firs, is now firmly lodged in my mind.

Today though, the weather is good, and the going easy as I rejoin the Icknield Way, in the correct direction, as it crosses into Hertfordshire. The broad path runs between hedges for much of the morning, climbing through woodland to Telegraph Hill and Deacon Hill before dropping back to its preferred lower level. Along the way, some excellent views to the north across the Bedfordshire plain. I get to the neat and tidy village of Pirton. A sign on the triangle of grass opposite the church says, 'Great Green, Permit Holders Only', which I feel is a tad possessive even for a great green. There is also a rather cosy bus shelter with several shelves of books (I wonder what this says about the service). I can't help but scan the titles; there's one called *The Perfect Man*, which I find a bit intimidating, then my eyes fall on *Nomad*. That's more like it.

A further two miles to the delightfully named Ickleford, where I stop for lunch. This would have been the endpoint for my last outing, but I am continuing for a few extra miles today. The first section post lunch is along pleasant field-edge paths. Then things become distinctly urban as the large town of Letchworth is reached and then neighbouring Baldock, where I catch the train home. On the journey, I reflect on how pleasant the day has been and how enjoyable the route is. Had I attempted this section last time, tired and wet, it wouldn't have been half as nice.

Baldock to Royston: 23 October 2019 (14 miles)

I love an adventure. Although northern Hertfordshire may not compare to finding the source of the Nile or climbing Everest's South Col, it's still jolly good fun. So, I set out today full of excitement and anticipation.

Once out of the town, enjoying this remote corner of the county: open farmland, wide grassy tracks across the hilltops, narrow footpaths winding through hedge-lined byways, and a few villages – not of the picture postcard variety but neat and functional.

I took a short detour at Wallington to visit George Orwell's cottage in Kits Lane. He spent the years before the war here, and it's where, it's said, he found the inspiration for *Animal Farm*. The village name, not heavily disguised, is called Willingdon in the novel.

Then it's a long section along a green lane, a narrow track initially between hedges, then crossing open farmland. Leading up to the farmyard, the path becomes deeply rutted by tractor tyres, the ruts filled with suspicious brown sludge. I greet a cyclist who passes me from the other direction. As he looks over his shoulder to return my hello, he falls off his bike into the 'mud'. Feel a bit guilty. Otherwise, the landscape is deserted, and I barely meet a soul all day. Perhaps the solitude set my mind, completely unbidden, to compose a prose poem, – 'What am I?' – exploring the physical and spiritual dimensions of existence. Mercifully there is insufficient space to include it here.

The last couple of miles descending into Royston were sublime, with 180-degree views across to the hills in the north and a wonderful sense of space. It lifted me out of my introspection to a broader vision.

Thirty years ago, I often worked in these parts and was sometimes tempted by the enticing footpath signs leading into the unknown. I did pull off the road more than once and do just that. But only a few hundred yards along the track, duty called, and I would reluctantly head back to the car. One day, I thought, I will come back.

Royston to Great Chesterford: 6 November 2019 (14 miles)

A large and striking direction sign is fixed to the wall of a building near Royston town centre. It has black lettering on a yellow background and reads 'Großalmerode 798 km'. A small blue plaque confirms what I'd already half guessed: it is Royston's twin town in Germany. Although I wasn't going that far, it still promised to be an adventurous day as I entered what I'm calling 'The Empty Quarter'. Had local guides been waiting outside the station, touting for business, they might well have turned away shaking their heads when I told them where I was heading

Much of the route was vast stretches of arable farmland, devoid of crops at this time of year and often with the footpath forming a strip of grass, making a dead-straight line into the distance. Also, big open skies, blue in the morning, fading to grey later. An immense feeling of openness and space. No people, besides a few souls in the villages I passed through, and no animals, the farmyards seemingly deserted.

Rather worryingly, the route passes close to the bullpens at Freewood farm, but even these are vacant. And later on, walking down an unfenced road that stretched as far as one could see, no vehicle passed. I was also struck by the silence; whenever I paused to check the map or for whatever other reason one stops, it was so quiet. Only the distant sound of aircraft flying in or out of Stansted. At times I found the morning a slog with its unswerving, uneven, and unending paths. Got much more into the feel of things post lunch and really began to enjoy this rather remarkable and slightly strange environment.

The further reaches of the Icknield Way will be tricky with poor transport links and will probably have to wait until next spring. But I might be able to squeeze one more section in before that, although it would mean an early start and would have the added peril that should I miss the 15.23 back into London, I would be faced with a four-hour wait at an unmanned railway station in the middle of nowhere, no coffee, no bun and in the dark. To ease the wait, a torch and book would be mandatory. It's tempting, though, very tempting

Great Chesterford to Dullingham: 20 November 2019 (20 miles)

It was always going to be a challenging day: very early start due to the distance from home, remote countryside, short daylight, and potential transport complications at the end. The walk itself was fine. Field-edge paths around wide swathes of arable land but with the trail occasionally making its glutinous way straight across freshly ploughed fields. And long straight tracks, green lanes they call them, cutting through the landscape and over the hills.

The sky was rather strange, reminiscent of failing light at the end of a long summer's day. Hard to know whether it was really getting dark or just pretending. A couple of minor navigational errors were soon corrected. The first was due to a wonky waymarker, and the other was a lack of concentration because I was busy making up a song when I should have been checking the route. It was pretty deserted, just a few small villages along the way, and for the first six miles after lunch, I didn't see a soul.

But I'd miscalculated the distance at 16.5 miles when it was actually 20. This meant some fast miles towards the end to beat the fading light and to give a chance of catching the 16.03 train from Dullingham to Newmarket, where there's a connection to Cambridge. Made it with minutes to spare. The prospect of a four-hour wait put wings on my heels for a fast final mile.

Dullingham Station is unmanned and lacks any useful information about arrivals or even which platform to wait on. When the train did come, it was just a single carriage. Battered and tired, its best days well past. Also, it was so crowded it was difficult to get on board, but there was no way I was being left behind, so I fought my way on. Soon at Newmarket, but the 16.19 to Cambridge never came, cancelled just minutes before it was due. Next train in an hour. And I was feeling cold, despite five layers, hat, scarf, and gloves. There was a shelter of sorts, with seats of sorts, but it was opened ended, and the direction of the biting wind made me feel like one of those model planes they test in a wind tunnel. I could at least lend my battery pack for someone's dying phone.

The 17.19 was also cancelled a couple of minutes before its scheduled arrival. I noticed a few of the passengers making their way to the station car park, and on impulse, I followed them, trying to look lost and desperate, and it worked! A taxi pulling away stopped, and one of the three passengers opened the window and asked if I wanted to share a taxi to Cambridge. 'Yes, yes, please,' I replied, fighting back the tears. Squashed uncomfortably against the nearside rear door for the 30-minute journey was of little matter. I was on my way home. And I did get home at 9.00 pm – almost 15 hours since starting out. Seldom had the prospect of a hot bath been more appealing.

And I know you are curious about the words to the song whose composition distracted me earlier in the day. So here is the completed version:

I'm walking on the Icknield Way, an ancient path I'm told
It's a bright and lovely day, but maybe a little bit cold
Got up early to catch the train, arriving in good time
Coffee and bun in the local shop and on the trail by nine

Up the hill but not too hard, it's all going rather well
What will happen later on, I really cannot tell
Across the fields, down the tracks, the views are really fine
Stop for lunch on a windy hill, I'm having such a good time

Nearing the end, and time is tight, must push the last few miles
Feeling fit, make the station ok, but not the end of my trials
The journey home was pretty bad, but on it, I must not dwell
Great Anglia Trains, sorry to say, you did not serve me well.

Dullingham to Icklingham: 28 July 2021 (19.5 miles)

At 5.30 am, the forecast was not promising. '70% chance of heavy rain and thunder early afternoon.' A little daunted, I decided to focus on the 30% chance it wouldn't happen – sort of glass three-tenths full mentality. I've been waiting over a year and a half to complete what was my third long-distance path, and I'm keen to be underway.

The long outward journey meant I didn't leave Dullingham Station until 10.00 am. However, the relatively easy paths and the flat landscape allowed me to make good progress.

Much of the route is through arable farmland going across or around large fields of ripening wheat. Whether this constitutes bread basket territory, I'm not sure. Not the spectacular views of earlier sections but big wide-open spaces nonetheless.

Around midday, I'm following a quiet road running gently downhill to the Suffolk border, the sixth and final county this ancient path will encounter when I notice ominously thick low clouds on the far horizon. Soon the trail leaves the road to follow the River Kennett for a mile, and I feel the first few drops of rain. It has also become rather dark and windy.

Now, I'm not too fussed about the rain or thunderstorms. But I'd rather not be crossing open countryside when they occur, and I began to feel uneasy. However, half an hour later, the skies have lightened, and the threat seems to have passed.

Post lunch, and the weather is looking good, I passed the point where I could have shortened the walk by several miles and didn't give the idea a second thought. A little further and The Way leaves its predominantly easterly progress to strike due north. A somewhat monotonous long, straight path along the side of another wheat field eventually met a wide track leading to woods that would take me to the village of Herringswell.

Pausing to look back, I could once more see those ominous clouds and what looked like heavy columns of rain not far away. The wind had strengthened as I walked through the woods, rattling through the treetops. A precursor of a storm, surely? Then the large raindrops began to fall, with enough force to warrant putting on my coat for the first time. But five minutes later, all was calm, and the sun returned.

Two miles from the end, I was enticed into a farm shop where I bought a can of drink and a tiny piece of cake. The lady asked me if I'd got caught in the downpour. 'No,' I replied a little smugly. 'I didn't.'

The last mile was along a broad sandy track, bordered by a wire fence supported by rough wooden posts. To the right a wildlife area with tall grasses and yellow flowers blowing in the wind. To the left, a view across scrubby low-lying ground to a line of trees on the horizon. Thick columns of rain hovered in the distance. It had the feeling of the Wild West or the Australian Outback. One might have expected it to lead to a frontier trading post, not the bus stop outside the church in Icklingham.

The journey home was something of a nightmare, a long wait for the bus to Thetford, then a train to Cambridge where I took the first London-bound train to depart – Thameslink to King's Cross. All well to begin with, then informed, 'This train will terminate at Welwyn Garden City due to operational difficulties', a euphemism for broken down, I suspect.

Although an alternative train arrived soon after, it wanted to stop at every town, village, hamlet, or crossroads in Hertfordshire, or so it seemed. The 'calling at' stations list barely finished before the next stop was reached. Got home just after 9.30 pm, having left at 6.45 am. A long but satisfying day.

Icklingham to Knettishall Heath: 4 August 2021 (19.5 miles)

Leaving home early and three trains and a bus later, I set foot on this last section of the Icknield Way at 10.15. The first four miles followed a broad track between plantations of cedar trees and were quite pleasant if a bit of a slog. I only meet one person on this stretch, but it is a fortunate meeting as he tells me the path is closed a mile further on and advises a diversion. Having found the alternative path, it's another mile through the forest on an increasingly sandy track until a main road is reached.

The trail enters a small wood on the far side, but the path is unclear. Two gentlemen of about my own age are coming in the opposite direction. They ask me for directions, and I them. We both know what's behind us but not what lies ahead. One of them had the appearance of an ageing hippy, a large man with thick grey curls flowing over his shoulders and halfway down his back. A bandana and a suitably outrageous T-shirt. However, he spoke with the cut-glass accent one might expect from a high court judge or the chairman of the golf club. Disappointed to learn they were not searching for a modern day Yasgur's Farm, merely the Black Horse in Thetford for a pub lunch.

After crossing a few fields and a short stretch of woodland, the path followed a broad, horribly sandy road for another four miles. Huge farming vehicles frequently forced me to step into the bushes that lined the road as they rumbled by. Having reached 11 miles, I reckoned it was time to stop for lunch. Rejecting a large pig farm as a stopping point, I settled for a log at the side of an enormous field where a cereal crop was being harvested.

Lunch could have gone better. Firstly, I was dismayed to find my John West 'Lunch to Go' Mexican Tuna Salad no longer comes with a small plastic fork. I looked for a fork substitute, not really being an eat with your fingers type. Remembered I had a multi-tool penknife thingy in my rucksack and used a combination of pliers and a small file for cutlery. Then, eating nothing more dangerous than a soft roll, one of my crowns fell out and into the long grass at my feet. Still contemplating another expensive trip to the dentist when the passing combine harvester sprayed me with dust and sand. Time to move on.

Soon reached the village of Euston, where another sandy track, three miles this time, would take me to the end of the trail (no vehicles now, just a rutted and tedious path). I reached the car park where the Icknield Way gives way to the Peddars Way, which runs 49 miles to the north Norfolk coast. A signpost pointing back the way I'd come informed me it was 105 miles to Ivinghoe Beacon, so I took this as the official end, having searched in vain for a promised plaque. I trudged my weary way back to Euston.

I didn't fancy the long wait for the bus to Thetford Station so I ordered a taxi for the first time on a Wednesday Wander. It was a tough day, with most of the walk on tiring sandy tracks and with little of interest to distract the mind. Still, completing the 200-mile adventure that started with the Ridgeway Path in Wiltshire and crossed south-east England to the Norfolk border was satisfying. Can't say I enjoyed every minute, but quite a lot I did.

Chapter Five

The Chiltern Way

When my walking adventures were mostly confined to the central Chiltern area mentioned in the introduction to Chapter Two, I sometimes puzzled over the Chiltern Way. I met it, running east to west, at Chorleywood and then again, some miles north near Wendover. Perhaps there were several footpaths with the same name? When I cared to investigate, the simple answer was that the two paths I'd encountered were on opposite sides of a circular walk. The more astonishing answer was that it had a circumference of 134 miles.

The route was devised to mark the Millennium and circumnavigates most of the Chiltern Hills area. In the following years, three extensions were added to further the coverage. The southern and northern extensions, plus the Berkshire Loop. I decided 134 miles were enough for now, and I'd concentrate on just doing the original route.

It should be noted that during 2023, the southern and northern extensions were incorporated into the main walk, but with an option to go via the Berkshire Loop on the southern section. Making a total mileage of around 176 miles whichever option you chose. I was using the 2016 version of Nick Moon's excellent guidebook on my walk; he was the creator of the route so one is in the safest of hands. The Ewelme Loop (walk four) is described therein but is not in the current version.

I started the project in January 2020, when the world held its breath anticipating the spread of the Covid virus. I'd done five sections of the walk, about 80 miles, when the UK lockdown came into force. Later in the year, when the stay local rule was partially relaxed, I restarted my walks. However, obeying the restrictions on avoiding public transport, I devised my own circular walks to allow me to drive to the start/finish point. Doing about 10 miles on the Chiltern Way before heading back via alternative paths. I did not write up the first couple of these, hence the gap between Princes Risborough and Wigginton in these accounts.

Hemel Hempstead to Coleshill: 22 January 2020 (18 miles)

As the guidebook suggests, I set out on my new project from the starting point of Hemel Hempstead Station. The dictionary describes the word dank as 'unpleasantly damp and cold'. It defines today's outing well. The sky is a grey blanket covering the landscape. A milky sun did make a brief appearance mid-morning but was quickly shunned by an ungrateful world that merely pulled the bedclothes up tighter.

The station's coffee kiosk looks like it served its last Americano some time ago. I have to make a detour to a garage on the bypass to get my drink and bun, so essential on a day like this. Then it's back past the station and under the bridge to find my first Chiltern Way signpost. I take a picture of it against the backdrop of the bridge brickwork and wonder what adventures I will encounter over the 134 miles of this circular walk before I'm here again.

The guidebook also assumes a clockwise direction, so that's the way I head. Shaking off the town's traffic noise and semi-urban grip takes a while, then the narrow path enters a large field, mist hovering over the hedge line in the distance. I feel immersed in the countryside once again. The first five miles were new to me, but much of the remainder were on paths already familiar from other walks. Down into the Chess Valley near Sarratt, across the river, and up the other side via a steep, slippery track to Chorleywood. Not too far, and it's down again into the Misbourne Valley and, inevitably, back up another steep hill. A further mile to Coleshill, where I left the Chiltern Way to reach Amersham.

But I mustn't complain about those steep-sided valleys because they both contain something of a rarity: a chalk stream. It is estimated there are only 260 of these in the world, and England has 224 of them, mainly in the south and south-east. We are fortunate indeed.

Although the day was rather grey and damp, it was still lovely for walking. A challenging distance with a few taxing and slippery hill climbs added in. I sometimes look forward to this sort of winter wander during my summer walks, but I would now be happy for it to be summer again. Such is the human condition.

Coleshill to Marlow: 29 January 2020 (15 miles)

This is a tale of perils avoided in my attempt to reach the end of the day unscathed.

The bus from Amersham dropped me at the junction with New Road just before 8.30. It should really be called 'Narrow and Twisting with no Pavement Road', for that's what it is. It leads gently uphill into the village of Coleshill. It's a bright but cold morning with frost and possibly black ice still lurking under the hedgerows at the edge of the tarmac. To avoid this, I keep more to the centre of the road while looking out for any cars whizzing around the bends. I reach the village safely and rejoin the Chiltern Way.

Pleasant open countryside for the first few miles, and the only peril at this stage was the possibility of an involuntary glissade down one of the muddier slopes. An equally lovely walk followed as the path weaved through the woods with helpful CW white arrows painted on a few trees. High Wycombe Golf Course came with a warning that I was crossing a golf course and to watch out for stray balls (in case I hadn't realised). I run the gauntlet of the fairway without incident and head across the main road to a tunnel under the M40 motorway. These things always make me nervous, and I'm glad to emerge into the sunlight at the other end.

Nearing the end of a long, straight stretch on a field-edge path, I see what I think is a walking group standing near the gate that leads to a lane. But as I get nearer, I can see it's a group of about a dozen men, all wearing green jackets and wellington boots, broken rifles across their arms, and dogs at their feet. They don't respond to my friendly greeting. Over the stile, along the lane, then up a narrow path towards the woods. Two ladies out walking their dogs do say hello but also advise me not to be alarmed at the imminent likelihood of gunfire further up the track. I seek refuge in the woods and find what I think is a safe spot for lunch. However, not out of earshot of the gunfire. I hope they missed, whatever their target.

More woods follow and are tricky to navigate. I'm relieved to pick up my first CW waymarker for some time, but less pleased that it directs me down a steep descent on badly worn wooden steps to the horribly busy Marlow Bypass. I double-check the OS map, which confirms I need to cross the dual carriageway and continue up the bank on the far side.

Even with the aid of a central reservation, it took several minutes and a certain amount of courage to achieve this. A scramble up the bank led to a metal gate with two cables in front of it connecting an electric fence on either side of the gate. I've met these before and know you must carefully unclip the wires and reconnect once through. That done, I find a labyrinth of electric fenced paths dividing the fields ahead. Left and right quickly led to dead ends but straight ahead looked more promising. Half a mile on, that too became impassable – the way barred by cables that could not be unclipped. No option but to retreat from this Kafkaesque scenario.

Once safely back across the road and up those dodgy steps, I had a rethink. OS maps are good at warning you of a danger zone, such as an army training area or quicksand, but could be better at more parochial matters. The guidebook, which I'd not bothered to consult, might be more caring. It was. 'You'd be stupid and lazy to cross here, walk half a mile down the road and use the underpass' is not quite what it said, but it might have done.

A hundred yards on, a grubby laminated card fixed to a lamppost reinforced the underpass advice. A few more miles and I'm in Marlow, where I thought about going on a little further, but passing a bus stop and with a bus to High Wycombe station due in five minutes. I decided not to ride my luck further and instead ride the bus.

Marlow Bottom to Nettlebed: 5 February 2020 (17 miles)

A damp and misty start to the day as I set out from Marlow. A climb through woods, where the mist swirled amongst the trees and the thick leaf mould provided a soft brown carpet to give the first mile an unworldly, intriguing feel. Out into the open, I paused to take in the westward view across varied farmland until the horizon dissolved into a haze.

By the time the lovely village of Hambleden was reached, the sun was out, and the visibility much improved. A fairly heavy bank of clouds hovered over the valley but nothing too threatening. After passing the Old Bakery and the church, the CW turns due north, which made me a bit grumpy as I'd prefer to be heading west. Or maybe it was just because of my dodgy ankle, an old running injury, that was having a moan. For this two-mile stretch along the valley bottom was nothing to complain about, with its broad and easy paths offering views across the river to the hills beyond.

When the trail turns east, I feel more justified in my displeasure. It was the opposite direction to where I was ultimately heading and the start of a woodland climb on an exhaustingly steep and slippery path. Having toiled to near the top, I take advantage of a nearby bench and stop for lunch. Had I carried on a few more minutes, I'd have found the path swings back to its original westerly trajectory and opens onto a stunning vista of rolling hills far into the distance. There was a perfectly placed bench which would have been a great lunch spot. Bit gutted.

A rare descent to reach a village whose pub boasts it has frequently been used for the filming of *Midsomer Murders*. Knowing the programme's reputation for bizarre plots, I imagined one involving bitter rivalries between local walking groups and the inevitably dire consequences. Moved swiftly on. Another climb up a grassy track looks back on Lunchtime Hill, as I'm calling it. I pause to catch my breath and appreciate the patchwork effect of the sun peeking between the clouds and illuminating the fields below.

An enclosed path leads to Stonor Park, a vast area of parkland surrounding an imposing country house with formal gardens, various auxiliary attractions, and, of course, a gift shop and tea room. But I don't stray from the high-level path that slowly drops to the road and onto the next stage of the walk to Southend. This one has no pier, and is about as far from the sea as you can get on this sceptred isle.

Around 4.00 pm, having passed through Maidensgrove, once reckoned the most remote village in the Chilterns, I'm back into open country, and with a few miles still to go, I realised I'd been somewhat over optimistic in how much can be achieved on what are still relatively short days. There was a real risk of losing the light before I finished, so finding the quickest route to civilisation became my priority.

The dilemma was whether to burn precious minutes studying the map or continue following the CW until a course became obvious. Decided on the latter, which paid off when a mile later, I came to the junction with the CW southern extension, which, if followed south for a mile, should get me to the outskirts of Nettlebed and a bus to Henley Station. Set out at a march, not daring to look at my watch for fear of discouragement. Made it ok and just a few minutes before the hourly bus arrived. Although not without an accusing sliver of moonlight striking the edge of the bus shelter to remind me of my folly.

The Ewelme Loop: 12 February 2020 (17 miles)

Understanding this south-west corner of the Chiltern Way is not easy. For this is where the main trail meets the return of the Berkshire Loop, the outset of the southern extension, the Ewelme Loop, the return of the southern extension, and the Russell Water Short Cut (official).

Luckily, the Ewelme Loop forms part of the original route, which is all I'm concerned about now. I read it can be omitted if one opts for the Russell Water Short Cut (official), but I'm glad I didn't. The loop starts near Nettlebed in South Oxfordshire, so that's where I head in my car. First, though, to the community café for a coffee and for one of the best cakes I've ever tasted – pear muffin still warm from the oven. Fully prepared, I head out the mile and a half to meet the CW and the start of the loop.

The combination of being distracted talking to someone and an ambiguous waymarker meant I took the wrong path but in the right direction. Two miles later, I met the correct path at a three-way junction and joined it there, so no harm done. The third path, I noted, was another way back to Nettlebed.

A pleasant walk through woods and a few quiet roads until the path climbs to a ridge with an expansive view across the Wessex downs. I stopped to take a picture and a drink, but a cold wind penetrated my multiple layers, gloves, etc. So soon got going. The path dropped down to Ewelme village, which is the point where the loop does a U-turn and heads eastward back to the start. With the last cottage left behind, a broad grassy path runs downhill with a view of Swyncombe Downs ahead, which we will soon be climbing.

With the stiff ascent completed, it was time for lunch. Sat on a fallen tree trunk with the slightly worrying look of a bear lying on its back, suspiciously offering its tummy as a bench. Safe enough, as it turned out, but it was still cold, and I was glad to be on my way. Views now to the north as the path slowly descended towards Cookley Green. A feast of wonderful but hard-fought-for vistas today.

Stubborn can mean tenacious (usually good) or stupid (which isn't). I like to think I occupy the hinterland between the two. I felt dissatisfied when I arrived back at the junction where the loop started and where I had initially taken the wrong path. I wondered if I could redo the first bit and then pick up that track to Nettlebed I'd noticed.

The first half mile on the now correct loop path was on a dreadfully muddy bridleway where the assistance of fence posts and trees was needed to keep on two feet. Relieved when the waymarker directed me across open meadowland, complete with grazing sheep. Got to a point where a large white arrow painted on a tree (common on the CW) could be interpreted as straight on or half left up the hill. Made the wrong choice which meant climbing over a few farmyard gates while hoping not to be chased off for trespassing. Soon I was at the three-way junction from earlier and the track to Nettlebed. This started ok but disintegrated when the path entered woodland. A confusion of white, painted arrows in all directions, any one of which might be the one I needed. The following 40 minutes were spent using guesswork, compass, intuition, and a will to survive until I blundered onto a minor road that led back into Nettlebed and the parked car.

Earlier in the day, I was amused by a woman calling at the top of her voice to her disobedient dog, 'WHISPER, COME HERE, WHIIIISPERRRR!'

Nettlebed to Princes Risborough: 4 March 2020 (17 miles)

This time last year, I'd never heard of Nettlebed. Now, it's my fifth visit. For now, though, it's goodbye as I strike north, hoping to make the Oxford–Buckinghamshire border by nightfall.

The Chiltern Way could have teamed up with its prodigious near neighbour, the Ridgeway Path. The National Trail would probably have provided the quickest and easiest route to today's destination. And although the CW will ally with the Icknield Way further on in Bedford, it remains independent for now. And I'm glad of it.

The route has many twists and turns, ups and downs, and slippery slopes. Sometimes it meanders through the woods, seeming to have lost its way, then emerges, if not into brilliant sunlight, at least a clear enough day to enjoy the far-spreading landscape with its valleys and hills. There was even a tunnel with a light at the end of it – under the M40 motorway at Stokenchurch.

On the far side of that tunnel, the dull but innocuous day turned for the worse as a chilled wind blew across the empty green that lined the main road. I spied a modern-looking octagonal shelter which should make a good lunch spot. If you accept the definition of shelter as 'A place giving temporary protection from bad weather or danger', then this construction failed miserably. The walls were made of a metal latticework that offered zero protection from the elements, temporary or otherwise. Not much more than half a sandwich into my lunch, and the rain joined forces with the wind to torment a cold and hungry walker – I might just as well have been inside a car wash.

The rain continued most of the afternoon and undoubtedly further deteriorated a slope so steep and slippery that I had to make leaps of faith between tree trunks and low-hanging branches to prevent an uncontrolled descent. Arrived at Princes Risborough Station damp but happy, still feeling good after a demanding day and once again just beating the light.

One thing that will remain with me is the kindness of some of the people I briefly encountered on my outward journey. The lady getting off the train at Slough who thanked me and wished me a good day because I helped her find her stop; the friendly rail employee at Twyford who said, 'Good morning, sir, nice to see you today'; the lady in Henley who stepped aside to accommodate my faster pace, wishing me a good walk, wherever I might be headed; and the young bus driver on the X38 who said he would stop for me in Nettlebed so I needn't worry about requesting a stop.

Circular walk from Wigginton 18 September 2020 (22 miles)

Feeling in reasonably good condition and having enjoyed coffee and bun at the excellent Wigginton Community Shop (sitting outside), I set off to do some serious miles – although 22 was a little more than anticipated.

All went well until the fifth mile when I seemed trapped in what I shall call the Ashridge Triangle, where I lost sight of the Chiltern Way in the Ashridge Estate woods. Whichever way I tried, the compass indicated north; maybe it was the nearby Bridgewater Monument disturbing the magnetic field or my incompetence. Who knows?

I sat down, and with my GPS tracker, OS map, and a Mars Bar, I worked out where I was and calculated that if I went due south, the CW must eventually intersect my path. With no tracks going my way, I just blundered through the trees, keeping an eye on the compass, which I hoped was now clear of the influence of the Ashridge Anomaly. Found the path and recognised it as the spot where I was lost on another walk a couple of years ago. On that occasion, I joined the Chiltern Way when I didn't mean to. This time I did.

Learn from my mistakes, you'd think, but picking up the pace after my aimless wanderings, I whizzed past a left turn where the 'Way' turned north. Half a mile further and realising my mistake, I turned back.

The Chiltern Way is not a single path but a clever connecting together of numerous existing ones to produce a continuous 134-mile loop. Sometimes they are broad and well-established trails, and at other times they are more obscure and less obvious. Therefore, abrupt turns are not uncommon, and a missing, poorly (or in one case wrongly) placed waymarker, or a not-concentrating walker can spell trouble. Anyone within earshot would have heard me loudly vocalising my self-criticism. Luckily there wasn't.

Back on the right track and calmed down, I managed the rest of the day without further incident. I stopped for lunch after 10 miles, at Studham, where I would say a temporary goodbye to the Chiltern Way for the day (and where I would need to return to next time). The stile where we parted looked fairly recently rebuilt and made an excellent picnic table, as long as no muddy boots appeared to squash my sandwiches. The route back followed first the Icknield Way, then the Ridgeway Path, a route I'd travelled in the opposite direction a year ago on a hot day, pleased it was a little more temperate today.

Walking along the wide ridge that leads to Ivinghoe Beacon, I stop to exchange a few words with a lady who's enjoying the view across the Vale of Aylesbury. She confesses to being a fan of Crowded House. 'I am, too,' I reassure. She then cites their song 'Four Seasons in One Day' as a suitable anthem for today's weather. It has been what the forecasters sometimes call 'changeable', but I feel this is a bit of an exaggeration. However, barely have the words left her lips when a weak sun is blotted out by a sudden squall of soft rain blowing across the exposed ridge, and I cannot disagree. Thought how I might slip the group's 'Weather with You' into the conversation, but fail to do so. Getting quite tired towards the end but pleased to have completed those serious miles without injury. I could have gone further – at least another hundred yards.

Studham to Chalk Hill: 9 October 2020 (15 miles)

Some days, most days, I feel enthusiastic about going for a walk. Today was the exception as I set out to do a few more miles along the Chiltern Way. It was a dull day weatherwise and arguably a section I didn't need to do. Not only that, but I'd have to do it twice.

Much of the route is shared with the Icknield Way as it crosses Dunstable Downs. I had done this lovely walk last year on an impeccably sunny day. Today I not only need to retrace those steps in less appealing conditions but also turn around at Chalk Hill and re-retrace those steps. There being no viable circular route. Still, if a job is worth doing as they say.

First, I needed to get to the finishing point from my last outing at Studham. But the nearest place I could find to park was two miles further on at Holywell. So, a two-mile walk to the start, turn round, and back along the same, not incredibly inspiring route past the car. A prelude to my more substantial double back later on. But that second route reversal did have compensations: a surprise view and a belated ice cream.

Dunstable Downs has one of the finest views in the Chilterns, even on a not particularly fine day. After passing the Chiltern Gateway Centre the path drops gently to my turn-around point, a couple of miles north of Dunstable's town centre. Coming back up that gentle descent, half an hour later, the trail morphed into a gruelling climb, and it all seemed a bit of a struggle. But a path followed in the reverse direction can offer a new perspective on the landscape, and this one, under the dome of a striking mackerel sky, made it all worthwhile.

The Chiltern Gateway Centre sits at the highest point and slightly back into the hillside. It commands the best view of all, an unimpeded vista of the Vale of Aylesbury stretching away to the northern horizon. Last year's visit was on one of the hottest days of the summer, when I stopped at the centre's café in search of a cold drink and an ice cream. The former was easily catered for but dismayed that the only variety of the latter was for dogs.

Today, approaching the near-deserted car park, I saw what I assumed was a fatigue-induced mirage. I prepared myself for disappointment, but the nearer I got, the more confident I became – a Mr Whippy van. An irony of sorts. I asked the friendly purveyor why he bothered on a day like this. 'Well,' he responded, 'if you stay home, you don't sell anything.' Pleased he didn't. Sitting on a bench, coat collar turned up against the strong and chilly breeze coming up from the valley, I decided my vanilla cone was worth the wait under this impressive sky.

Returning to the car, I took a minor diversion to revisit the Whipsnade Tree Cathedral. Had it to myself and, wandering between the various chapels and transepts, bathed in the strange light that found its way through the trees. It was an atmospheric and peaceful visit. I was glad I took the time. The next section will pass the 100 mile mark on my protracted journey, but more importantly, I hope to reach Sharpenhoe Clappers. The place has no particular significance; I just like the name.

Chalk Hill to Upper Sundon (and back): 23 October 2020 (17 miles)

I wanted to do a few more miles along the Chiltern Way but knew it wouldn't be an easy day, nor particularly interesting; when the Sundon electricity substation, the sewage treatment works, and the M1 motorway are some of the landmarks, maybe it doesn't bode well. But it needed to be done if I was ever to complete the circle of the Chiltern Way.

Set out from Chalk Hill, just north of Dunstable, a little before 9.00 am, fortified by a large coffee and a sausage bap. The first thing to negotiate was the extensive diversion around a vast housing development north of Houghton Regis. It had been met on the Icknield Way last year, which shares this part of the route, but work had advanced considerably since then, and diversion notifications appeared at regular intervals. They warned of walker-prohibited routes sanctioned by the Secretary of State for Transport. Undoubtedly, I breached these, but I'll let you decide whether it was one man's futile gesture of civil disobedience or a lonely walker disinclined to turn back.

Despite a few other local diversions and delays, I reached Upper Sundon by late morning, having completed 10 miles. I hoped to get as far as Sharpenhoe Clappers, which has become a bit of an obsession, but sudden and very heavy rain – a cloud burst, they used to say – made me think again. A couple of cyclists had already occupied the village bus shelter, so I turned back with some reluctance and a desire for dry trousers. At least I'd achieved 100 miles on the Chiltern Way when I passed the Red Lion pub. Ten very wet minutes later, the rain stopped, and the sun came out, which was annoying in a funny way. One path I trod not half an hour ago was now more stream than footpath. Got to a point where the Icknield Way, which had been sharing the path, took a northerly route while the CW went south. Thought it would be more fun to take this alternative way back, and, despite a few tricky bits, it worked well.

The best part of the day was just before reaching Upper Sundon. A bowl-like dip in the terrain, not filled with trees as one might expect, but bushes of many shapes and sizes displaying all the colours autumn can muster, from bright yellow to deep golden brown. The footpath weaved down between the well-set shrubs before climbing again to reach the village.

The search for the still elusive Sharpenhoe Clappers continues.

Upper Sundon to Luton: 30 October 2020
(15-mile circular walk)

I didn't think I'd get a walk this week until British Gas phoned to reschedule my 'anytime between 8.00 am and 5.00 pm' appointment because they'd forgotten they had a stocktake. I seized the opportunity.

Started walking around 8.30 from a spot just north of Luton. The first objective is to return to Upper Sundon, where I left the trail last week. Unfortunately, this meant going five miles in the wrong direction, which was disheartening. Some of this was on paths I would shortly be returning on. I tried to take only brief glimpses of the view so they could surprise me on the way back. Very windy at times, and my OS map briefly found a new role as a sail. Thought I'd managed to get it refolded correctly, but later found it was upside down.

Keen to get to the intriguingly named Sharpenhoe Clappers, which I failed to reach last week, I was encouraged by a smart metal fingerpost, green with a yellow arrow at the tip, stating it was a mile away. Even then, it proved elusive until I stumbled upon a small car park. And there it was, the place name boldly displayed on a weather-worn sign. Nothing there, really: one picnic table and a few trees with a good view beyond. Even the car park admitted it was small and advised people to go away if they couldn't find a space.

A long descent on a zig-zagging path with panoramic views across central Bedfordshire was the highlight, maybe only rivalled by Warren Hill at the end of a most enjoyable day.

In several places, the path was shared with the John Bunyan Trail. I'm pleased to report that this pilgrim did make progress with another eight miles done on the Chiltern Way. This leaves just 25 out of the 134-mile route to do. The figure-of-eight route I'd devised to return to the car meant visiting the village of Streatley twice. It may not have greatly resembled Bunyan's Vanity Fair, but I did manage to resist its temptations on both occasions.

Luton circular walk via Breachwood Green:
4 November 2020 (22 miles total)

Today's outing had the potential to be an excellent day's walking, but it would be something of a challenge at 22 miles, requiring an early start.

The alarm is set for 5.30 am, out of the house at 6.30, and on the trail just before 8.00.

I picked up the Chiltern Way from last week's finishing point, just north of Luton, with a climb up Warden Hill. Fantastic early morning views across the town and beyond on a frosty day with clear skies. A mixture of emotions, joy being out on such a beautiful morning, and the prospect of my first walk on entirely new paths since March, but also much sadness at all that is going on as we face another lockdown from tomorrow.

Anyway, time to negotiate the tricky descent along narrow, slippery paths. Still wearing gloves, not so much against the cold but as protection should I stumble. Once on level ground, I could enjoy the route as it made its way around the eastern edge of Luton, briefly visiting North Hertfordshire before turning back into Bedford. Mainly across gently undulating and open countryside, visiting quaintly named villages: Lilley, Butterfield Green, Mangrove Green, Peter's Green, and my favourite – Tea Green. All these are linked by field paths, quiet lanes, and tracks, plus the ancient green lanes prevalent in these parts.

After 14 miles, I reached East Hyde and the end of the Chiltern Way for now. From here, the Upper Lea Valley Walk will take me into Luton from the south and ultimately back to my car a few miles beyond. It's an easy trail, at least this bit is, built on a disused railway line and is on mostly level and firm ground. Then it dumps me in the centre of town. A torrid experience with a confusion of walkways, bridges, and flyovers while I struggle to find the A6 exit going north. Getting very weary towards the end and relieved to reach the sanctuary of my little car.

Memories of the day? A bench near the top of a steep hill on the way to Lilley, the now bright sunshine illuminating rolling green hills that stretched into the distance. A perfect spot for 'elevenses', but due to the early start it was 'nine-forty fiveses'. And a lone tree in the middle of a large field, overseen by a moon still just visible in a cloudless sky. Only 13 miles to go of my protracted Chiltern Way project, not much more than a half day's walk in normal times. I don't know how or when I can do it, but I'll be back.

East Hyde to Hemel Hempstead and back:
14 April 2021 (24 miles)

I have been so, so, so (one more), so excited at the prospect of a long walk this week. The relaxation of the stay local rule has allowed me to complete the last section of my 134-mile Chiltern Way project (although it took 235 miles of walking to achieve this). It's over a year later than expected, and five months since my last visit.

I hit the trail at 9.00, having enjoyed a second breakfast and relishing the prospect of the untrodden footpaths and unseen vistas ahead. A narrow lane takes me to Harpenden, then through several alleyways until the first proper footpath is reached. Shortly after this, the CW joins the Nickey Line Trail, a disused railway that runs seven miles from Hemel Hempstead to Harpenden and will provide a shortcut for the return leg. But for now, we're on it for less than half a mile before turning west and following the edge of the last golf course of this venture.

A little further on, the River Ver is met (last seen on a walk to St Albans). The river leads towards the unwelcome but necessary crossing under the M1 motorway. This is an unnerving process, crossing the slip roads leading to the motorway and walking in front of the protecting barriers. Glad to leave that behind and head uphill across a large field filled with yellow flowers and onto the village of Flamstead.

Now the path turns south-west through mostly deserted countryside as it heads towards Hemel. Steeply downhill to a winding path through a water meadow on the River Gade before the last hill climb of the Chiltern Way. The summit makes a good lunch stop; on the northern horizon are the Sundon Hills I walked the previous autumn and, somewhere beyond that, the much-anticipated Sharpenhoe Clappers. Soon I hit the Hemel Hinterland as open farmland gives way to light industry and housing estates. And it's only a little further until, once again, I'm standing by the footpath sign beside the railway bridge, where I started my adventure one misty morning in January last year. The circle has been completed, and I'm pleased.

It's taken exactly 14 miles to reach this point, but I plan to reduce the return leg to around 10 using my Nickey Line shortcut. Unfortunately, it lies on the other side of town. The two-mile trek through the centre makes me wearier than I would have hoped, and it takes some willpower to ignore the line of taxis waiting for fares. I fall into more of a rhythm after the first few miles on the Nickey. I'm glad my pace hasn't dropped and grateful that railways, even erstwhile ones, generally avoid hills. A little further on, I bump into Peter, an old friend, cycling towards Hemel. We stop and chat for a few minutes, and this spurs me on for the last few miles back to the car.

Driving home, I contemplate three things: a lovely but challenging walk; the completion of another long-distance path, albeit protracted; and the chicken casserole I put in the slow cooker before leaving home – hoping I remembered to turn it on.

'Footnote'

This is the last outing for my old boots before they receive an honourable discharge from active service. One thousand five hundred miles walked, including four long-distance trails; they have served me well and deserve mention.

The Berkshire Loop

Beaconsfield to Maidenhead: 27 July 2023 (20 miles)

It's over two years since I finished the 134 mile Chiltern Way original route. Now that the northern and southern extensions have been subsumed into the main walk and the Berkshire Loop given as an alternative option, I felt I had some unfinished business.

Being a new route (to me) meant my mind was occupied with taking in unseen vistas and keeping a close eye on the map; there was no time for the introspection that could dominate a familiar path. It had more hills than I imagined but was also lovelier; often, the two go hand in hand. The latter stages, though, were problematic. Firstly, when the waymarker directed me through a turkey farm that made it very clear it did not welcome visitors, then a longer than planned trek into Maidenhead in the rain.

After crossing the bridge at Cookham, the trail loops through a pub garden and under the bridge to join the Thames Path. I enjoyed the quiet and tranquil paths of the morning but did not enjoy this busy mile long river section very much, and I'm relieved when the walk turns away to climb Winter Hill – even if it does require crossing a golf course. There are some unexpectedly lovely views across the valley before reaching Pinkneys Green, where I leave the Berkshire Loop to get to the station in Maidenhead.

Minimal research (i.e., the cursory read of the guidebook) had left me imagining Pinkneys Green as an idyllic patch of well-manicured grass next to a church, a parish noticeboard, and maybe just enough room for a bench. What I found was a vast open space of grassland with a footpath curving into the distance through the long grasses.

The two-mile trek along the A4 Bath Road into town was unpleasantly tedious and tiring, especially when it started to rain. I called into a small supermarket, bought coffee, and a packet of end-of-the-day reduced price sandwiches. A little further on, by some traffic lights, there was a small patch of grass with a bench. I sat on the damp seat, with the rain running down my face, but still enjoyed my mini feast. Perhaps this was the nearest I'd get to the Pinkneys Green of my imagination.

Maidenhead to Henley: 22 September 2023 (13 miles)

Today's weather was suitably fickle for the equinox; one metaphorical foot still tentatively lingering in summer, the other firmly entrenched in autumn. Leaving Maidenhead Station, the air was warm and clear, if not actually sunny. Then a tedious two miles along the A4 Bath Road to rejoin the Chiltern Way where I left it last time. Astonishingly, the bus that serves this busy road only runs on Saturday, so is no help to me, or anyone else living around this well populated residential area, who doesn't want to wait until Saturday.

The morning is mostly spent threading through woods or along narrow paths at the edge of woods. Around lunchtime, the route emerges into wide-open countryside. It seems to be getting a bit dark, and when I turn to look behind me, I can see that the fluffy benign clouds of earlier, each happily sailing along in its own space, have huddled together into a menacingly dark bank of malevolence. I think I might get away with it, as the columns of rain seem to be away in the distance. But no, soon the first raindrops are felt, and before I can get my coat out of the rucksack, I'm getting uncomfortably wet.

After half an hour, the sun is out – just in time to enjoy the path that dissects a vast deer park that gently descends to the Thames. The route is defined by frequently placed wooden posts; the well-trodden grass clearly visible as it sweeps downhill. Views across the valley to the hills beyond complete this beautiful scene. Young deer scatter away as I approach, not knowing that I mean them no harm. The CW joins the Thames Path for a mile before turning away from the river in favour of a cross-country climb to Henley.

I'd been searching in vain for a lunch spot and settled for a redundant stile. The sun has obligingly stayed out, and the stile acts as a combined bench and table, with the post as a backrest. It's peaceful here with just birdsong and the warmth of the sun, and I stay a little longer than necessary. A couple more miles shouldn't be too taxing, though, in such nice weather.

Reaching a sunken woodland path, it starts to rain again. Then there's a flash of light above the canopy of trees, followed by a long peel of thunder that resonates across the sky. The rain becomes heavier, and the thunder more frequent. It's all a little unnerving. I arrive at the outskirts of Henley, damp but relieved. Ready to start the long journey home.

Chapter Six

The Greensand Way

When I was walking the North Downs Way, I had often pondered the high ground that seemed to be following a parallel path a few miles to the south. I discovered it was the Greensand Ridge, and like the North Downs, it runs across Surrey and Kent but this time stopping short of the coast by finishing on the Romney Marshes. Then I found out there was a Greensand Way.

Guidebooks were hard to obtain. I could only find one. Written in 1997 and presumably now out of print, I got my copy from a second-hand book dealer. It is a beautiful book with thick glossy pages, much information about the area you will walk through, intricate route maps, and detailed directions. But its nine-inch square format makes it more suitable for the coffee table than the trail, even with map-accommodating trouser pockets. Imagine an oversized Mr Men book. At the time, the only other information I could find was some notionally updated route notes produced by Surrey Council and similar ones for Kent. Both largely based on the guidebook. Since then, the Surrey section, at least, has been fully updated.

Waymarkers were sporadic: good on some sections, absent at crucial points on others. This, plus some inept and lazy navigation on my part, produced some interesting results. As you will see. The Greensand Way may not be as well known or high profile as some of the other long-distance paths, but it was one I greatly enjoyed, possibly my favourite.

Haslemere to Shamley Green: 25 August 2021 (22 miles)

The long-distance route starts at an alleyway between shops along Haslemere High Street. It has a nice green plate on the wall to mark the occasion. But Surrey Council, perhaps in a pique of parochialism, has only seen fit to direct us to the Surrey border at the appropriately named Limpsfield. 'Greensand Way 55 Miles' it states, but there are another 53 in Kent to the walk's official finish at Ham Street. Maybe they just put 'Here be Dragons' beyond their eastern boundary.

The path quickly climbed to Hindhead Common, with expansive views across the countryside and a late summer fecundation of purple heather. Soon at the summit of Gibbet Hill, with new vistas to enjoy across the Devil's Punchbowl – the vast natural depression that lay below.

My out-of-date guidebook and the Surrey Council route notes directed me down a narrow path leaving Gibbet Hill. They said I was to carefully cross the A3 London to Portsmouth Road and take the footpath opposite. There was no road, a wide sandy track, possibly a cycle trail, but no road. It felt right to turn right, so I did. Although it was the correct way to go, it did lead to some navigational folly a little further on. I now realise, as I should have done then, that the road was beneath my feet in the impressive Hindhead Tunnel.

I'd walked 16 miles when I arrived at Hascombe and was struggling a bit. I had hoped to do another four miles to Shamley Green, but a series of tough hill climbs and steep descents had been a shock to the system after my recent outings on the flatlands of East Anglia. The guidebook indicated a bus from here, but my search for a bus stop was unsuccessful. Like the A3, it may have gone underground. No choice but to carry on.

I was reasonably sure I'd followed the instructions correctly which directed me towards a sandy uphill track that would lead into woodland. I was not initially over concerned by the lack of waymarkers; these things happen. Often, it's prudent to turn back when a mistake is discovered, and sometimes best to keep going and find an alternative route. A runner approaching in the other direction confirmed I was not on the Greensand Way, but if I turned left at the track T-junction, it 'should' lead to it. A horrible descent on probably the worst sunken track I've ever encountered; a narrow and stony path with a two-foot-deep trench running down the middle, as if a malevolent claw had decided to make an already tricky path even harder.

Figured it was safer to be in the trench than fall into it and scrambled my way down to the single-track country lane beyond. Followed this for a mile to emerge at a main road and the possibility of working out where I was. But it was the A281 – the busy trunk road that runs between Guildford and the south coast, and it didn't cater for pedestrians. It was beyond the edge of my map, but I thought going north was the best option. I was soon rewarded by finding the sanctuary of an out-of-town retail village. It was deserted. Had there been grass growing between the cracks in the pavement, I might have thought for decades. However, it was probably only vacated half an hour ago - when the last bus left. No option, then, but to keep going north.

Now it was deciding between the ankle-wrenching verge, thick with tall weeds and riddled with potholes, or chancing the edge of the road facing the oncoming traffic. Chose a combination of the two, assessing the relative dangers as I went along. An anxious mile later, I arrived at a turning into a farm. Now able to locate it on my map, I could see the possibility of a three mile route, much of it on a disused railway line, that would get me to Shamley Green.

The extra miles were not welcome but infinitely better than staying on the road. With half a mile to go, I paused at a road junction to check the way into the village. 'Still looking at the map?' I looked up to see the runner I'd asked directions from over an hour again. Too tired to cover my embarrassment with a witty remark, I just asked for confirmation that I was heading the right way.

Shamley Green was just that, a large expanse of grass incorporating the cricket club and leading to the bus stop. I was greeted by a gentleman drinking from a tin of beer, and not his first of the day, I guessed. He announced what the electronic display had already told me. That a bus was due in 10 minutes. There was a corner shop opposite; time to get a cold drink. Thought about asking my fellow traveller if he wanted anything, but then I thought better.

Luckily, I'm not a purist in these matters and don't feel the need to walk the bit of the route I missed. So, I'll pick up the next section from the bus shelter and see how things go.

Shamley Green to Dorking: 3 September 2021 (18 miles)

A gentle beginning on a level footpath soon becomes a more challenging terrain: minimal level ground but many climbs and descents, the latter often on deeply eroded and hazardous sandstone gullies.

When the trail entered the extensive woodland area of Hurtwood, I felt sure the fern-lined twists and turns of the path would lead to trouble. The waymarkers were sparse, and the correct route was pure guesswork amongst the numerous alternatives, each with a valid claim. Relieved when I got to 'Hurtwood Control Car Park No.1' as the guide notes required. I'd already visited car parks 3 and 4 and wondered how many Hurtwood car parks there are (14 is the answer).

This whole morning of challenges led to one place, Leith Hill. This is the highest spot on the Greensand Ridge at 965 feet and the second highest point in the south-east, being beaten into the silver medal position by a mere 11 feet by Walbury Hill in Berkshire. But The Leith Hill Tower, built by an eccentric Georgian gentleman, reclaimed the highest spot at over 1000 feet. Surely that's cheating?

The area around the tower was quite busy, possibly with the tail end of the summer holidays. Still, I found a bench to myself and enjoyed a well-earned lunch, but the promise of a spectacular view to the South Downs was thwarted by haze.

The predominantly east-going path now turns due north for the next few miles and provided the only navigational misdemeanour of the day. I followed the sign for Wotton, which was the correct direction for the Greensand Way, but I was off the trail. Knew this when the path that threaded downhill through woodland, denuded by logging activity, met a road that shouldn't be there. Did some metaphorical head-scratching as I followed the road for a bit until reaching a turning that swept steeply down into the woods again. Didn't fancy climbing back up, so very relieved to find my first Greensand Way marker since before lunch.

A little further on, the unusual sight for Surrey of a waterfall. It was on private grounds but could be spied through a gap in the hedge. It must be significant, as it's marked on the OS map. So, another post-lunch first, I knew I was on the right trail and exactly where I was on it.

The GW turns back to its easterly direction after Wotton and heads for Westcott and on to Dorking. Things become increasingly urban as the town centre is approached. You might have hoped for a short walk across town, picking up some refreshments before reaching the station a little to the north-east. But no. The trail markers, so elusive earlier in the day, emphatically direct south of the town and up a long climb into

Glory Wood. A short section through the edge of the woods and the path does a U-turn back down the hill, eventually dumping you on the busy A24, which must be followed for another mile to reach the station.

Honestly, at this end of the day, I'd done enough climbing and visited enough woods, so I found this two mile diversion at the least unnecessary and, at worst, sadistic.

One strange encounter during the morning was meeting a pheasant standing in the middle of a woodland path. I stood still, some way off, to take a picture before it fluttered away. But I needn't have worried, for it began to follow me, close at heel like a dog and squawking as it went. It would frequently switch to the other side with similar behaviour. I couldn't decide whether friend or foe, but after a few hundred yards (and it was that far), I found it a little unnerving, and when the path started uphill, I increased my pace. The bird gave up at this point and stared at me as I pulled away. I felt a pang of remorse that I'd let him down.

Dorking to South Nutfield: 8 September 2021 (12.5 miles)

My first two outings on the Greensand Way have been quite adventurous. Physically demanding in the miles done, hills climbed, and navigational challenges.

Today it seemed appropriate to take things a bit easier. The landscape and the walker need to calm down a bit. The former does this by not being the North Downs Way which runs a parallel route no more than a couple of miles to the north and is already toiling up the steep slopes of Box Hill. My part in this more relaxed day is to finish at a sensible point and not push those extra miles just for the sake of it. To reach Oxted (20 miles) would be nice but might be unwise or over optimistic. We'll see. It doesn't mean there weren't any hills, there were, but the total ascent today was a modest 776 feet compared to 2,072 last time.

But what the route lacked in breathtaking views was compensated for by a very pleasant, easy-to-follow rural walk crossing farmland and narrow lanes through functional villages and parkland. The walk's highest point was Reigate Heath – ancient heathland that dates back 4,000 years. I imagine the golf course and the windmill that sits above the clubhouse were a later addition. Things became more urban on reaching Reigate but soon out to more countryside and via a bit of a dog leg to South Nutfield.

It was only 3.00 pm, and although there was a train station a few hundred yards down the road, I was sorely tempted to continue onto the next station at Oxted. This would have been a good eight miles away, and for once, prudence won over folly, and with some reluctance, I called it a day and waited for the train to Redhill. Maybe the 'Just be sensible' message is beginning to sink in, but not too deep, I hope. An incident-free trek across the Surrey countryside on new ground? Yes, right now, I'll buy that.

South Nutfield to Westerham: 15 October 2021 (14 miles)

Trainline's email confirmation for my journey seemed impressed by my choice of destination. 'You're going to Nutfield and Upper Warlingham!' it announced enthusiastically.

They obviously knew a thing or two as it was a lovely walk with plenty of interest and some excellent views to the South Downs. But it was also a day with more navigational difficulties than my pride is prepared to admit when the map, route guide, waymarkers, and how I saw the world failed to agree. And if all that wasn't enough, it's also border country. Comfortable Surrey giving way to the wilds of Kent, or maybe it's the other way around? One of the more unusual things I passed was a bath. Quite a nice one, a kidney-shaped shiny white one. It sat near the edge of a field, a blanket of leaves covering inky black water and two empty Coke tins floating around the vacant tap holes. Tempting.

The 55-mile Surrey section of the Greensand Way ends near Limpsfield and not far from Crockham Hill (I'm not making this up). But I'm going a little further to the more positively named Goodley Stock. After nearly a mile through woodland, I come to a six-way junction. The map confirms this is the county border, but all is quiet, perhaps too quiet? A wooden post with finger signs indicates the multiple options of paths, one of which should be the way I need to go.

It could be the action of nocturnal agents, I don't know, but the signs are poorly aligned, and it takes me three attempts to find the correct path to the road. Even then, it was an uncomfortable mile along a narrow pavement-less lane to get to Westerham, where a bus would take me to Oxted Station. I should leave the Kent bit until next spring, but I may not be able to resist a little further folly before then.

During the last leg of the train journey home, I reflected that despite a very early start and a strenuous day's walk, I felt pretty good and confirmed my mental image of still being only 27. Then a young lady stood up, looked at me kindly, and asked if I'd like to sit down. Not wanting to repel her kind gesture, I accepted.

Westerham to Sevenoaks: 27 October 2021 (15 miles)

The shrill, insistent noise fills my head, the room, and possibly far beyond. Bewildered for a few moments until I realise it's just the alarm beckoning me out of a fitful sleep. But, looking at the clock, why 5.30? Of course! It's adventure day.

Determined to make the most of the final Wednesday before the dreaded going back of the clocks, I'd planned to walk the first Kent section of my Greensand Way project, and an early start was imperative.

Exactly four hours later, I'm stepping off the bus in Westerham. All seems quiet and peaceful but, to be sure, I pay homage to the area's best remembered resident – great statesman, amateur painter, and part-time bricklayer. And there he is just a few yards from the bus stop. This unusual and larger-than-life sculpture has Mr Churchill sitting, a little uncomfortably perhaps, on a chair that rests on a large slab of limestone. A small plaque tells me that it was given to the town in 1969 by Marshall Tito on behalf of the Yugoslav People.

That done, and I'm on my way. Pleased to find the signage is, in general, much better than the Surrey section. This leaves me free to concentrate on the hill climbs (of which there are many) and to enjoy the long woodland paths punctuated by open hillside with some great views to the south and a sprinkling of neat Kentish villages.

Later in the day, there's a long stretch of farmland to cross. Tricky terrain and, in one case, tricky livestock. I've crossed a particularly wide and muddy field when I discover my exit is blocked by some rather grumpy looking cattle. I stride through, but I deliberately don't make eye contact for fear of becoming fainthearted.

On my last walk it was a bath, today it's a metal table and chairs making an incongruous appearance in the countryside. With traces of the once vivid green paintwork still clinging to the elaborate fretwork, the furniture sits under the canopy of a tree. Thoughtfully placed as a potential picnic spot, perhaps. Shame it's too early.

During some of the most challenging climbs, I hear Sir Winston enjoining me to 'Keep going, never give up.' And again, I hear him while waiting for the train at Sevenoaks. Now he's seated, and after taking a long pull on his cigar and then a generous slug of whisky, he says, 'It should be perfectly possible to get another section of your walk done before the winter sets in.' Then, just as he raises his glass again to his lips, I think I hear him mumble, 'Maybe more', but I could be mistaken.

Sevenoaks to Yalding: 3 November 2021 (14 miles)

I decided I could squeeze in one more section of the Greensand Way, despite the challenge of an hour and a bit less daylight since last week. After all, I have the requisite map, compass, and torch, and I'm told there is a whistle somewhere amongst the many straps and buckles on my new rucksack, although I'm yet to find it.

Catching the 8.09 from London Bridge got me to Sevenoaks and a visit to the coffee shop in time to be on my way just before 9.00. The first couple of miles were fast and easy walking, initially across the town centre, then through the deer park. Leaving plenty of time for more testing and remote parts later on.

But let's not move on too quickly. It's a clear day with a heavy frost. The deer park is almost magical, with the frost still lying in the shady hollows and a bevy of does with their fawns grazing in a patch of sunlight near the cover of trees. The path leads across a broad and long tract of land lined on either side by woodland, but there's no wind, and the sun brings a little warmth, welcome on this nippy day.

After such a positive introduction, you might expect this report to slip into a tale of woe and tribulation, tricky terrain, navigational nightmares, or flooded fields (all have featured in previous wanders), but you'd be wrong. Just a few dilapidated stiles and a bit of difficult route-finding, nothing to spoil a lovely day for walking with the early morning mist and frost giving way to sunshine and a gentle breeze.

Mid-afternoon, the sky became overcast, and ominous rain columns gathered on the horizon, but they didn't come my way. And by the time I got to Yalding, a late afternoon sun cast the long shadow of a weary walker across the field, a reminder that the days are indeed short as winter approaches. A fingerpost, directing left to continue on the route or right for the station, brought a pang of regret. I reluctantly turn right and bid farewell to the Greensand Way for now. 76 miles done, 32 to go. Had I been Captain Scott, I would probably have built a hut here to over-winter in before setting out next spring – possibly laying a food depot at Platt's Heath. But I'm not, so I went home for a warm bath and tea.

Last time it was a table and chairs set out in the woods and before that, a bath. Today's find was perhaps the strangest of all; an eclectic collage of items assembled outside a forge. Amongst them, a metal rooster sitting on a milk churn (bearing the name Beadles Forge), a giant clay fish, a horse-drawn plough now painted a fetching powder blue with red wheels, an industrial-sized mangle in similar livery, and a skeleton riding a baker's delivery bike.

Yalding to Lenham: 20 April 2022 (17.5 miles)

'Crossing the Medway Gap' is the title my route guide gives to this section, creating an enticing whiff of adventure. At the beginning of November, I had 32 miles left of this long-distance path before bad light stopped play. With the longer days afforded by British Summer Time, I'm very excited to be back.

We might return to what the Medway Gap is, but the River Medway itself was traversed shortly after setting out. My previous crossing, further downstream, had been on the high-level, kilometre-long Medway Bridge, which the North Downs Way shares unequally with the M2 motorway and looks down upon a wide riverbed 40 metres below. Today's crossing was less dramatic over a low brick bridge on a narrow country road, but still an excuse to celebrate. Captain Scott would add a half-inch square of chocolate to the evening rations to mark significant occasions during his journey to the South Pole. Had there been a Village Tearooms on the summit plateau, as there is in Yalding, then I feel sure he, too, would have called in for coffee and cake.

I ordered my Americano and contemplated which delicacy to choose when the friendly assistant asked, 'How about a slice of lemon cake? You look like a lemon cake sort of man.' Not sure how Scott would have reacted to that (he was more a Pemmican sort of man), but it was spot on for me – my favourite flavour and my favourite colour all in one not-so-small package. I sat outside at a small table on the modest forecourt, enjoying the sunshine and contemplating the day ahead.

The first few miles were through an expanse of open countryside with impressive and mostly unimpeded views towards the South Downs. But it was also deserted, and if it hadn't been for the cultivated fields and well-kept orchards, I might have thought the tearooms a time machine that had propelled me into a post-apocalyptic landscape. It reminded me of watching the children's TV programme *Mr Benn* when my daughter was growing up. Each week he would visit his tailor and be kitted out in suitable attire for his adventure before being thrust out of the backdoor into whatever scene awaited. But just in case you worry that the end of the world is an unsuitable subject for young minds, rest assured, it did not feature. Even so, I would not have been surprised to see him rushing back before the portal closed on his 20-minute exploit.

Later on, the orchards would become prolific, covering acres of ground. Mostly the footpath ran to the side, but on a couple of occasions it was directed between the rows, a sort of Hampton Court Maze with apple trees and signposts. Sutton Valence reminded me of learning about valence bands in semi-conductor theory, something to do with electrons jumping about when they get excited. Well, I was excited following the path that runs high above the village, looking over a jumble of roofs and buildings to the southern hills beyond. But still shackled by social inhibitions, I didn't jump. The only navigational folly was mistaking Chart Sutton for Chart Hill, an annoying pre-lunch additional mile.

And what of that Medway Gap? Well, depending on where you read it – it's the product of a primeval landscape when the river cut through the chalk deposits, a meeting of several road and rail links, or a collection of posh villages with expensive houses. Take your pick.

Lenham to Charing: 4 May 2022 (17 miles)

Several people know I like walking; a few even consider I'm good at it. If you fall into the latter category and don't want to be disillusioned, please don't read any further. And likewise, if you are in the former group and wish to spare me embarrassment, there's no need to continue. For the sake of complete disclosure, though, I feel I must make a record of my day with its tale of woeful incompetence unparalleled since my Thame Valley Walk misadventure. If you've decided to keep reading, please be kind in your judgement.

No problems with the train to Lenham or the two mile walk to Boughton Malherbe, where I'd left the route last time. The first two miles on the Greensand Way to Egerton should have been similarly trouble-free; the map shows it as an almost straight path running south-east.

Crossing a stile overgrown with nettles, on which I didn't avoid being stung, led to a large field that ran downhill to a hedge. Couldn't see any waymarkers, and given only two choices, I turned right. Seemed the correct direction, and after a few minutes, I began to congratulate myself on my dead-reckoning navigational skills in the absence of signposts.

Then I got to a road and a village I wasn't expecting. Grafty Green, I now know it to be, but not at the time. However, Church Road was signed to a place name I recognised as being on the route, but I stupidly didn't check the map. I just followed the road. A mile uphill slog that got increasingly deserted brought me to a T-junction and the church that the road name promised. Swept by a wave of despondency and frustration when I realised it was Boughton Church, and I was back in Boughton Malherbe, where I'd started the walk an hour ago. Three miles walked to get nowhere. No wonder the name was familiar.

Over the stile again and the ignominy of getting re-stung by the nettles. Tried left this time, which went a little better, but once again dumped me on a road I'd not expected. This time a signpost to Egerton gave more hope of progression, but it was a long detour. My ambitious plan was to get to this long-distance path's finishing point at Ham Street. The best I could aim for now was getting to Ashford, leaving about 10 miles to do next time.

You'd think I'd made enough errors for one morning, but not so. Leaving Egerton by the recreation ground, I took a wrong straight-on; that is, I didn't turn left when I should have done. Across an increasingly rough farm track until, guess what? Another road. This time it was on a sharp bend, making it easier to find on the OS map but no less depressing as yet another tedious detour would be needed to meet the footpath.

I Stopped for lunch in a rather uncomfortable spot in the woods and considered my options. Realistically there was only one: get to Little Chart and take an official two-mile Greensand Way link route to Charing Station. Annoying, as things had started to go much more smoothly. This is painful to admit, but if I hadn't gone wrong, it would have been only six miles to Little Chart – I had walked fourteen.

The first part of the link route was along a quiet lane until it met a busier road at a junction. The marker directed me across the road into a vast stretch of open land with a narrow path leading around tall grasses or crops. I couldn't decide which. After half a mile, I realised the trail was taking me in the wrong direction, turned around, and forged a way through the two-foot-high grass. Encouraged that the contours of the land matched the OS map, I pressed on. Nearing the road that would take me to the station, I stopped to look at the map for an exit path. As I was doing so, something prodded me in the back. I looked around to find three ponies, each keen to do more prodding. I reached a metal gate and quickly shut it behind me. Whether they were being friendly or seeing me off the premises, I don't know, but they gathered around the other side of the gate staring at me, and I felt I'd spoilt their fun.

Little Chart to Ham Street: 25 May 2022 (15 miles)

On 9 January 1909, Ernest Shackleton failed to reach the South Pole. He got within 97 miles when dwindling supplies and sickness forced him to turn back. His 'Farthest South' would remain so until Roald Amundson rather sneakily beat Scott to the pole in 1911.

Likewise, my efforts to finish the Greensand Way on my last outing were unsuccessful. In homage to the great explorer, my diary records the botched attempt as 'Farthest East'.

Let's see how today progresses.

5.15: An early alarm for this final and farthest flung stage of the Greensand Way.

7.20: At St Pancras Station, waiting for HS1 to speed me to Ashford International. Then it's the all-important coffee before a short bus ride to the walk's starting point at Little Chart.

9.20: And I'm on the trail. Setting out on a previously untravelled route is always exciting, each bend offering something new: a splendid vista, a delightful woodland path or green lane, or the less welcome steep hill, muddy field, or invisible footpath.

13.10: Ten miles done and time for lunch – I settle for a bench in the churchyard at Kingsnorth. So far, the terrain has been a mixture of heath, farm, and parkland. A few tricky bits, otherwise uneventful.

16.15: Despite the trail's best efforts to prevent me from finishing the walk with its overgrown paths, broken stiles, misplaced signs, and an unexpectedly muddy track through Ham Street Woods, I've made it. But there is some debate about exactly where in Ham Street the route ends; some say (rather conveniently) it's platform 2 of the station, others that it's a few hundred yards further on at the crossroads.

Like the blues singer Robert Johnson, 'I went down to the Crossroads.' But there's no plaque to mark my achievement, not even a Haslemere 108 Miles fingerpost. I sit in the small public garden opposite the Ham Street Dental Clinic and console myself with a coffee and some fairy cakes bought in the village shop. As I fiddle to reset my sports watch, a 'Back to Start' screen appears with an arrow pointing upwards. A device with a sense of humour. Clever.

17.02: I'm boarding the local train to take me to Ashford International, contemplating another adventure completed and already planning the next.

Chapter Seven

The Hertfordshire Way

The London Outer Orbital Path is known as the London LOOP. On the same basis, this walk could be called the Hertfordshire Hoop, which has a certain ring. The Hertfordshire Way, as we had better call it, is a 195 mile path that circles the county. I'd got excited about doing the walk after seeing a 'Hertfordshire Way Long Distance Path' sign when doing the Chiltern Way near Luton.

The best time to start the project would have been spring, but I had unfinished business on the Greensand Way then. Could I get a few sections of this new challenge done first? I thought so. This is why I set out from Tring Station early one morning, at the beginning of a particularly soggy February. The Hertfordshire Way guidebook starts the walk from Royston, but as this is the furthest point away from me, and the days are short, beginning this circular route nearer home worked better. Hopefully, the best countryside could then be walked in early summer.

Tring to Kings Langley: 2 February 2022 (16 miles)

After leaving Tring Station, I soon crossed the familiar ground of the Ashridge Estate, heading for Berkhamsted. But a surprise awaits me at the south-west corner of Berkhamsted Common, and it sends a tingle up my spine and a tear to my eye. I soon learned that the labyrinth of deep ditches in front of me were training trenches dug for soldiers before they were sent to France during World War One. A sense of the tumble of emotions these young men must have felt as they prepared to serve their country is almost palpable as I stand and gaze. Many would never return. I carry on my walk in a thoughtful mood.

Reaching Berkhamsted Golf Course, a decision has to be made. Whether to turn left as the 2005 Hertfordshire Way guidebook (second edition) and the OS map would have me do, or follow the waymarker and the Ramblers' Association notes to go right. I chose the latter despite misgivings about ignoring the hallowed OS map. It led into the town and onto the Grand Union Canal for a couple of rather tedious miles.

Leaving the canal path at Bridge 149 and turning right to the main road, I noticed the alternative route coming over the bridge from the left. It's been difficult to get hold of the latest version of the guidebook (third edition, 2017). The chairman of the Friends of the Hertfordshire Way Society and co-author of the book has kindly arranged for me to receive a copy. Maybe that will clear the matter up.

My pleasure at leaving the towpath is short-lived as the path climbs to a hilltop golf course. The climb doesn't bother me, but facing another golf course does. The guidebook warns that although the way not be obvious, it does run somewhere near the fourteenth tee. The best I manage is the second green, where, luckily, an opportunity to escape opens up, and I'm on my way to the village of Bovingdon, where I shall stop for lunch in the churchyard.

More than adequately refuelled, I'm on my way to Chipperfield Common, where I take a short detour to follow a sign to the Spanish Chestnut Tree. After a hundred yards, I find a large, dead-looking tree in a clearing. I ask a passer-by if this is the Spanish Chestnut Tree. They don't know but think it might be. Might be is good enough for me, so I take a picture and move on. Another two miles along field paths and lanes get me to Kings Langley and the train home.

It was a most enjoyable day, and I am looking forward to many further adventures on the Hertfordshire Way or the HW as I'm sure it will become. This is also a common abbreviation for hot water, and how much of that will I get into before I'm finished?

Kings Langley to Potters Bar: 2 March 2022 (18 miles)

Setting out from Kings Langley Station, the prospects for the day didn't look good. Grey sky, cold, and the threat of rain. A few hundred yards up Station Road, I passed the impressive Art Deco frontage of the Ovaltine Building, the stonework reflecting the colour of the malted milk drink, whether intentionally or not, I do not know. But it's just a façade behind which a modern development of flats lurks. The site produced its last jar of the elixir many years ago, and anyway, it's coffee I need, not a bedtime drink.

Like many of the towns I visit on my travels, the station is a good way out from the town centre, but visit it I must. I chose an independent coffee shop that served great coffee but in a disappointingly small cup. Although the accompanying *pain aux raisins* was marked as 'Superb' in my pastry-ranking system. Then it's back past Ovaltine, across the road, and down Milk Farm Lane. Most of the area was a hinterland for the factory, so its name is no coincidence.

Since my last outing, I have received the latest edition of the Hertfordshire Way guidebook and learned that the route diversion I followed last time had been imposed due to access difficulties. I also learned that there is a substantial alteration to this week's section due to safety concerns. Glad it came in time as once again the OS map shows the original route.

This south-west corner of the Hertfordshire Way is where it dips its toe into the shallows of suburbia, coming within a couple of miles of the old Middlesex border, now Greater London.

Many tributaries (if I may extend the watery metaphor) need to be bridged, crossed, or tunnelled under on this walk: motorways, trunk roads, rail links, and an actual river or two. It won't be a quiet neck of the woods, to test your metaphor tolerance to its limit.

On the edge of Watford, I enter Bricket Wood. A place I have passed signs to many times but have yet to visit. It is a hugely impressive place with wide, easy tracks running between the trees, occasionally breaking out into clearings and open spaces. But it has started to rain, and it's cold and damp. I concede I'm not seeing it at its best.

The rest of the morning is spent following footpaths across farmland and green spaces, through villages, and along quiet roads. Motorway noise is never far away, but I'm still in awe of those who pioneered such a rural path through this chaotic corner of the metropolis.

A couple of miles outside Shenley, an uphill path follows the right-hand edge of a field, and it is spectacularly muddy. There was a point when the track swung left and immediately right while ramping up the gradient. I just have to stop and laugh. I'm barely making any progress;

every step of territory gained is almost wiped out as I slip back down. But I succeed, and reach a level, tree-lined path that leads into town. Along the way, I find a bench that will make a good lunch spot. Opposite is a small pond or very large puddle, not sure which. I now have to decide whether to get a bus from Shenley and call it a day or carry on for another five miles to Potters Bar Station. With some misgiving, I choose the latter.

The onward path skirts around the town in a neat curve before expelling me into a desolate windswept landscape, the faint path running uphill into the distance. Once the hill had been conquered, the last few miles were easy and flat but somewhat taxing at the end of a long day. As I strode along the final half mile link path to the station, I hoped my future self would appreciate the effort I'd put in to facilitate a good start next time.

Potters Bar to Broxbourne: 9 March 2022 (16 miles)

Potters Bar is a relatively large town, and it takes a mile to reach my first footpath and a further mile to reach Northaw, a much smaller habitation but one with an impressive church. St Thomas a Becket sits majestically at the far end of the triangular green, and it evokes a 30-year-old 'I've been here before' memory. I'd been working in the area and was driving along the narrow country lanes to find somewhere to stop for 20 minutes to eat lunch. I had almost given up, when I saw the church. I can't remember whether it was the imposing building or a particularly dramatic episode of *The Archers*, but it stuck in my mind.

Past the church and down the lane for half a mile to another footpath that would take me to Cuffley. The path turns off to the east before reaching the town. A vast tract of agricultural land fills the view at the end of the short, narrow path that passes under the railway viaduct. A big decision is necessary here, but it's one I've already made. The Hertfordshire Way signpost offers two options: turn left to Hertford or right to Hertford. Left is the original route that runs north for 13 miles to the county town. But an alternative, much longer route goes east to Broxbourne, then north-west to Hertford, a total distance of 28 miles. I'm going to do it all: to Broxbourne today, from there to

Hertford next time, then back to Cuffley for the original route the time after that. That's what you need to do to complete all 195 miles of this long-distance path.

It's a long, gradual, and somewhat tiring climb to Goff's Oak, then through Hammond Street, before reaching the best part of the day. The HW passes through four consecutive ancient woodlands – so vast that (including my lunch stop) it takes two hours to cross, and I meet not a single soul in all that time. I like to think that was because of my pioneering spirit. It was more likely that they knew the middle section was a quagmire – defined in the dictionary as 'a soft boggy area of land that gives way underfoot' and it certainly did that. A half mile of the narrow footpath only being detectable by the occasional marker post rising above the squidge, it's no wonder people were giving it a wide berth. But the dryer paths were a delightfully liberating experience, winding and undulating their way between the bare trees and crossing streams and gullies on sturdy wooden bridges.

Enjoying the solitude, I think I might have a go at singing. Unwisely, I chose Van Morrison's *Summertime in England*. It's a song I like, but it was described by one critic as an embarrassing 20 minute rant. It doesn't go well, and the squirrels dive for cover. My version only lasts 30 seconds and the embarrassment is only between me and the wildlife.

Arriving on the outskirts of Broxbourne, the trail does its best to join me up with the New River for the last half mile, and to the steps that lead to the station. But the devious twists and turns down alleyways and sections of woodland needed to achieve this get the better of me, and I end up on a long residential road to the same effect. The New River is neither new nor, in the accepted term, a river. But I expect you'll hear more of that next time.

Broxbourne to Hertford: 16 March 2022 (13 miles)

Chancing my arm against a dire weather forecast that predicted heavy rain from mid-morning onwards, I made an early start to catch the 7.53 from Liverpool Street, a direct connection to Broxbourne. By 8.30 am, I was climbing the steps outside the station that led to the path on the New River. Most of the route switches between this and the Lee River

Navigation, and although I'm intrigued by the former's history, both are too canal-like for me.

The New River is a 28-mile man-made waterway built in the early 1600s to bring much-needed fresh water to London (and still provides nearly 10% of London's drinking water). It was half funded by King James I, whose displeasure could be expected if you polluted it in any way. However, it didn't stop him from falling into it, head first through the ice, in January 1622. Built 150 years before the first canal, it is an astonishing feat of engineering with a fall of just five inches per mile.

A small canal might be the best way to describe the waterway at this point, and we follow it for a couple of miles as it weaves behind housing estates and commercial property. Then, it's a switch to the River Lee Navigation for just over a mile until reaching Standstead Abbotts. This is a great relief as I'm getting a little bored, and it's here that a four-mile diversion offers the opportunity to explore the Ash Valley. As I step off the towpath and onto the High Street, it begins to rain. A few minutes later, and even with my proclivity to understatement, I must admit it's quite heavy.

But by the time I'm through the town and onto the footpath, and much to my surprise, it has stopped, and the sun is shining, the water dripping from the trees and bushes, glinting in its rays. The path follows the valley's top until descending to meet and cross the river Ash via a rickety wooden bridge. A muddy field takes me to a section of a disused railway, enclosed by overhanging trees, and then to open paths and lanes that will reconnect with the Lee less than a mile north of where we left it at Stanstead Abbotts. Just before it does, my phone pings. Not a message or WhatsApp notification but a news flash. I expect many of you got the same one and will never forget where you were at the time. It gave the brilliant news of the release of Nazanin Ratcliffe after so many years imprisoned in Iran. Such good news in a troubled world. This adds to making the Ash Valley adventure the highlight of the day. The path now resumes its alternating Lee/New River route.

An early start and a relatively short section mean I arrive in Hertford by early afternoon. Now, the rain is persistent and set in for the day. The county town has two stations – Hertford East and Hertford North. It's the latter I need, which is a shame as it's on the other side of town and proves elusive despite getting directions from a traffic warden.

I get to the station feeling damp and a bit frustrated, I succumb to the temptation of a second lunch and buy a cheese and onion pasty from the station shop and a cup of coffee. The platform shelter is rather basic, but I don't care. Suddenly, life seems good again. This was the second part of the alternative and extended route between Cuffley and Hertford. Next week, I plan to return to Cuffley to do the original course.

Cuffley to Watton-at-Stone: 23 March 2022 (22 miles)

Having completed the 28-mile alternative route between Cuffley and Hertford, I'm back to do the original one. Hertford lies almost directly north of Cuffley, and if one were to take a direct route, it would only be about six miles. However, the Hertfordshire Way makes a bit of a meal of it by taking a lengthy detour to the west, which doubles the mileage. Perhaps to allow the walker to visit several charming mid-Herts villages. Rather appropriately, the most western of these villages is called West End.

After finishing its meanders, the route takes a decisive northerly course as the path is squeezed between the edge of a band of trees and the fence bordering the mainline railway. The remnants of recent tree felling littered the way, and it was a tiring slog of just over a mile, and I wanted my lunch. But the prospect of sitting on an uncomfortable log while the 13.32 to Cambridge thunders past is unappealing.

Reaching Hertford from the south-west, it's a further mile to the town centre initially via a very steep residential road. You may have noticed a trend by householders who, rather than just throw stuff away, place items on the pavement outside their property (I got a coffee machine that way). I'm flagging, hoping someone has left out a chair, or even better, a settee, that I can use – even an old bedside cabinet would do. But no, I struggle on and, crossing a stretch of semi-urban open ground, come to the back entrance to All Saints Church. There must be a bench here, and there is. Grateful to find it and plonk down. I sit for a few minutes and enjoy the feeling of not walking. Then I get out my sandwiches.

Time to go, but as I stand up, my legs have stiffened to a point where the walk to the exit is a passable imitation of Boris Karloff's depiction of Doctor Frankenstein's monster. A bit of a shock for any passers-by, considering I'm walking through a graveyard.

I could, of course, call it a day and head for the station – especially as I now know where it is. But I don't. Instead, I follow the route north of town towards Waterford Marsh and the River Beane. I plan to follow the river for six miles until turning off the HW for a two-mile path to Watton-at-Stone Station. My tired legs appreciate the easy-going, flat, riverside path.

Crossing the Beane on a narrow footbridge brings me to the extensive Woodhall Park Estate. Sheep are grazing on either side of the river, scattered liberally across the grasslands. The path comes to a T-junction and a signpost. One finger pointing left, the other right. Neither have an HW marker on them, and as the left path seems to point back the way I've come and not in the direction of the town, I ignore it and take a right.

The baa of a few sheep is a pleasant reminder that you are in the countryside. A whole flock is something else: the bizarre vocal warm up of a mass choir maybe? I turn to look. I'm faced with 50 or more sheep who stop and stare at me, and I stare back. Walk on for a minute and turn again. A strange version of Grandmother's Footsteps. Now sheep are joining from the other side of the river, bottlenecking on the bridge. It must be a hundred strong now, and the baa volume has increased accordingly. Perhaps they think I have their tea in my rucksack. I shook them off by upping my pace and slipping onto a side path.

Passing a large and very grand house with 'No Public Access' signs prominently displayed, I carry on to the estate's boundary and an unusual ladder stile to get over a six-foot wall. Encouraged to see a Hertfordshire Way sign attached to the woodwork. Through a thin band of trees, I can hear a busy road and go to investigate if it could be an alternative road to Watton, but it's far too busy and dangerous to contemplate. Realising I've come too far, I head back to the signpost (mysteriously, the sheep have gone). Now trying the left path to see where it leads. It soon turns to the direction I'm hoping for, and a couple of miles later, I'm at the unmanned Watton-at-Stone Station and on my way home.

Watton-at-Stone to Bishop's Stortford:
30 March 2022 (20 miles)

I'd done my research. Arriving at Watton-at-Stone, I headed for the Crumbs Café for my pre-walk refreshment. The coffee was good, and the *pain aux raisins* unusual and rather excellent, resembling a knotted piece of rope. It was both delicious and substantial. Even if I did no more today, it would have been worth the trip.

The area is just a few miles south-east of Stevenage, but you'd never know. So remote does it seem. A couple of miles to rejoin the Hertfordshire Way at Woodhall Park, then back to the ladder stile I encountered on my last trip. Over the six-foot wall and onto a narrow path running east, parallel to the A602 cross-country trunk road. The usual point to cross this busy road was closed due to roadworks. I had to make a detour, then run the gauntlet of a traffic-light-controlled contraflow, walking on the road in short bursts when the lights were red and taking cover for the next opportunity. I was pleased to be past this and leave behind the noisy highway and its challenges.

Much of this walk was beside rivers: the Beane, Rib, Ash, and even the Dane End tributary. In between were the essential ingredients of a country walk: woods, narrow lanes, and pretty villages. But there was also a unique surprise waiting in the wings. First, though, I use the opportunity of a wide and flat tree stump to stop for lunch, there being ample room for me and my rucksack. Not a particularly attractive stretch, with the river temporarily hidden from view and a somewhat uninspiring landscape, but it would do.

I've often regretted not walking a little further for a more suitable lunch spot, and perhaps never more so than today. Shortly after setting out again, the HW ran through the corner of a small picnic area. 'Only for use by ticket holders', the sign announced. But the benches were deserted, as was the adjoining car park. Then I saw it. In the far corner, an abstract sculpture to take your breath away. About 10-feet tall and in three sections, it might best be described as a strange alien bird-like figure breaking out of a shell. Others may give it an entirely different interpretation. I approached in awe and reached out to touch the smooth metallic surface of this spellbinding structure.

As you may have guessed, I had stumbled upon the Henry Moore Centre. The place was opening for the season the next day, and one might have expected a bustle of activity in preparation, but no, I had it to myself. I couldn't go into the main grounds but could spy through the fence three more strange and captivating sculptures spread across the well-maintained lawn. Back at my original find, I stood under the semi-circular structure, and all external sounds seemed to disappear. I tried a tentative, 'Hello.' This was swallowed up as in a recording booth, but in deference to Sir Henry, I didn't try singing – something I would regret as soon as I walked on. I'm sure he wouldn't have minded a line or two from 'Sergeant Pepper'.

A few miles further, walking through a small village where the houses were set back from the road, a man called out, asking if I was ok and wanted a glass of water. I often forget to stop for a drink, and I took this as a timely reminder and accepted the offer. He seemed shocked when I told him how far I'd come and asked with concern if I had food and if I intended to walk along the busy road further up. I reassured him on both counts, although in truth my food supply was exhausted. I thanked him, and marched on. The outskirts of Bishop's Stortford were reached, and with a bit of difficulty, so was the station.

Waiting for the train, I'd forgotten about the vagaries of Greater Anglia Trains and my Newmarket Nightmare two years ago, until a message flashed onto the display panel saying 'The train is delayed due to a train fault' and it all came flooding back. The silver lining was that the delayed train was reassigned directly to London. I felt a bit sorry for those who wanted any of the 150 stops it had been due to make, but not as much as I should have.

Bishop's Stortford to Barkway: 15 June 2022 (20 miles)

When I started this project four months ago, the land was still in the grip of winter; it was cold, wet, and often spectacularly muddy. I did the first 100 of the 195-mile route before taking a break at the end of March. Now I'm back to do the second half, and the skies are blue, the sun hot, and the earth baked.

The route now leaves its easterly trajectory and heads north for a bit. The vista also changes to expansive open spaces in a largely deserted landscape. The endpoint was a bit fluid, with an outside chance of getting as far as Royston but a more realistic view of finishing sooner. I had trouble finding the bus from Bishop's Stortford to the start of my walk at an out-of-town Tesco. But, as usual, people are only too happy to help if you ask them nicely.

My first objective was to get to Stamford, and although it's only 12 miles, it did give me options to finish there and catch a bus to a rail station if necessary. It was an option I didn't take, but instead, I did something out of my regular routine – I went to a pub for a pint. Justified on two counts: firstly, there was nowhere else to eat my lunch; and secondly, I needed a drink after an enjoyable but tiring morning.

As the afternoon progressed, more gently rolling hills and wide paths through ripening crops. The route also crosses the disused USAAF Nuthampstead Airfield from World War Two. Parts of the cracked concrete runway remain visible through the crops now sown across the area. Not so much swords into ploughshares as B-17 bombers into tractors. But also, runways into motorways as most of the concrete was used as hardcore for the M1.

The weather was glorious and much appreciated, but also somewhat sapping on the energy. When I got to Barkway, I knew it was time to stop. There was a bus due in 25 minutes that would take me the remaining five miles to Royston. It was uncomfortably warm waiting for the bus, and I had to compromise between occupying a shady corner of the shelter and still looking out for the bus in case it was early. It was a small Hopper bus with only one other passenger. The driver was a bit impatient as I fumbled with the card reader and monosyllabic when confirming that the bus did go to the station. However, riding the rattles and bumps as we sped along the country lanes, head against the window and half dozing, was sublime.

The bus made something of a tour of Royston before stopping in what seemed a side street. The driver switched off the engine, opened the doors, and turned off the lights. After half a minute, I walked to the front and timidly asked about going to the station. 'That's me finished,' said the driver. 'Turn right at the end of the road, and the station is on the left.' The attendant at the station was much more forthcoming when I asked about the fare to Zone 6, from where I could use my Freedom

Pass, and came with me to supervise my interaction with the ticket machine. Again, if you ask nicely (most of the time).

Barkway to Baldock: 29 June 2022 (22 miles)

My Hertfordshire Way adventures have reached the far north-east corner of the county. This area contains some of the most remote and inspiring scenery the walk can offer. It promises to be a good day, as well as a challenging one.

I got to Royston in plenty of time for my bus connection to Barkway, where I left the walk last time. Sitting on a wall by the bus stop, I've time to enjoy coffee and cake bought from a nearby convenience store. 'That looks good,' comments a passer-by as I make inroads into my Belgian Bun.

The No.18 Hopper sped along the country lanes, and soon I was getting off in Barkway. I'm always impressed by the expertise of country bus drivers who hurtle along narrow lanes that I would think twice about taking a car down, and I told him so. He seemed pleased, and as I believe he was the same driver who'd been a bit grumpy last week, it was a nice bit of closure. The five mile route back into Royston was mainly across flat farmland until a missed left turn provided an alternative path to the town. This unplanned route ran uphill through the middle of fields of poppies, stretching in all directions. A serendipitous mistake.

If the town has a definitive centre, it must be the Royce Stone. Glacial debris and 900-year-old landmark, undoubtedly. Megalithic portal, as some would have it, maybe. It also marks this circular long-distance path's official finish (and start). But as I began the walk at the other side of the county, it was merely a convenient stop for water, and when there's no one in earshot to say, 'I've finished, so I'll start.'

Turning west out of town, the path soon begins the climb to the top of Therfield Heath and its view north to the flatlands of Cambridgeshire. But it's also where the fun starts as the path enters the wooded hilltop and splits into multifarious trails. With a dearth of waymarkers, I had to guess at the various options for half a mile until I met a gentleman coming in the other direction. He confirmed I was on the right track and gave advice for the path ahead. I mentioned the lack of signage, to which he responded, 'Oh, Barry looks after this section. I'll have a word.'

The next few miles were through wide open spaces of heathland that maintained the superb northern vista. One section had a warning notice that I was entering a rifle range and should stick to the path – especially if a red flag was flying. Coupled with an earlier sign on a golf course that warned about the risk of Serious Injury, I began to worry. Safely across, I stopped for lunch on the village green at Therfield and contemplated that I still had 10 miles to go.

The countryside became calmer with a succession of arable farmland and small villages. I realised I was committed to completing the total distance as the only village with a bus service was not expecting the next one until Monday – five days away. The route passes George Orwell's cottage at Wallington, last seen on the Icknield Way. On that occasion I had to take a diversion to visit 2 Kits Lane, this time the route passed the front door.

The last couple of miles into Baldock were across open countryside. Halfway along I came to a fence which had two identical metal gates, about 20 metres apart. Both had footpath signs: one pointing straight ahead, the other left towards a path that ran along the top of the field. While pondering the map, I saw a man leave the top path and walk in my direction. He looked like a country gentleman with requisite green waxed jacket, and a pair of black Labradors at heel. I was worried he was the landowner and about to tell me I was trespassing, but he couldn't have been more friendly or helpful, nor his dogs better behaved. He confirmed that straight ahead was the way to the town and advised I use the intermittently visible church steeple as a guide.

Walking up the High Street towards the station, I passed a fish and chip shop offering a portion of chips and a cold drink for £3. Resisting the temptation, I carried on a hundred yards until another shop offered the same deal. This time, I succumbed.

Baldock to Chapelfoot: 6 July 2022 (15 miles)

Today's walk saw the transition from the quieter parts of North Hertfordshire towards the large towns a little to the south-west. In the case of Stevenage, one could call it a conurbation.

The torturously winding track retained a rural feel – especially the early miles through farmland, woods, villages, and green lanes. Luton planes toing and froing were the only reminder of life beyond the footpath. Later there are large fields of ripening corn, some with narrow paths squashed at the edge and others almost excessively wide and boldly running through the centre of the crop.

The countryside persists almost to the edge of Stevenage, but added to the soundscape is the roar of motorway traffic and the intermittent whoosh of metropolis-bound trains, one of which will convey me to King's Cross later in the day.

I had planned to leave the Hertfordshire Way at a point where a three-mile route would take me to Stevenage Station. But enjoying a long stretch that made its way lazily downhill to a country lane, I missed the turning. Crossing a stile on reaching the road brought me opposite the Rusty Gun pub. Looking at the map, I could see that this was Chapelfoot, and the only way to return to my missed turn would be back up the path I had just enjoyed descending.

Next to the pub was a bus stop which offered the opportunity to catch an imminently due bus to Hitchin. Although this was one stop further up the line from Stevenage, I accepted the offer enthusiastically. As I stepped out at Hitchin town centre, I congratulated myself on a smart move, catching the bus here. Soon, I felt a little less smug when I discovered getting to the railway station required a mile walk along a busy main road, the pavement thronged with recently escaped school children. And not smug at all when waiting on the platform as the London-bound train whizzed by, next stop Stevenage.

Chapelfoot to Codicote: 22 July 2022 (8 miles)

You may have heard of, or even seen, *The Play That Goes Wrong*. Well, today was the walk that went wrong. This was a production in two acts. The dramatis personae for Act One are gathering at a bus stop in St Albans. The Second Act will essentially be a one-man show.

It required a 45-minute bus ride to get to my relatively remote finishing point from last week. If all goes well, I will be back in St Albans by the end of the day. I stroll to the bus stop with plenty of time to spare, and gradually others join the queue; a stout man (let's be kind) dressed in black has much to say to his lady friend, also in black, and anyone else in earshot. Then there are the two elderly French ladies dressed flamboyantly in multi-coloured leggings and long, flowing cardigans, and lastly, a tall thin man in an ill-fitting grey suit. Two or three others joined as extras to this increasingly Agatha Christie-like plot.

A few minutes before the bus is due, one of the French ladies wanders off to Poundland. Her friend, getting anxious, requests a search party to find her. Two of the extras are despatched, and they, too, fail to return. I'm thinking of wormholes in the space–time continuum, but that would be mixing genres. But all have safely returned when the Hopper bus pulls in, and we start to board.

I'm second up the steps and ask the driver for a ticket to the Rusty Gun pub. 'No idea where that is,' he says tersely. I'd forgotten the map called the place Chapelfoot, but I don't know if that would have helped anyway. I looked to my fellow travellers for help, all I got was, 'The driver can't be expected to know every pub on his route,' from the man in black, looking around for acknowledgement and appreciation from the others. I pointed out the Rusty Gun was the official name of the stop on the timetable, but that didn't help. Eventually, the thin man in the grey suit suggests I buy a ticket to Hitchin, which is the final destination for the bus. I acquiesce, buy my ticket, and sit behind the front seat. I was gratified when I heard 'No idea where that is' said to the next passenger.

As we set off, I realised I had become an involuntary audience to the stout man in black and his partner, who have sat in front of me. He had an opinion on everything from frying pans to flying saucers (I may have made that bit up). A lady boarded at the first village out of town carrying a large purple laundry basket. As she made her way to the back seat, her only lines were, 'Sorry, so sorry, can I squeeze through? Oops sorry.' Whether just a bit player or the late entrance of the main protagonist, I never discovered.

The problem with travelling on an unfamiliar bus route is knowing when to ring the bell for your stop. Occasionally, the driver is helpful, like the young Eastern European guy in Henley, who said I needn't worry, he'd stop at my destination. Obviously, I wasn't going to get any help like that today, so I tried to follow the route on the timetable I'd printed.

As the bus approached a T-junction with a major road, the tall thin man in the grey suit leaned forward and tapped me on the shoulder. 'When the bus turns left, your stop will be a few hundred yards on the left.' So, he did know after all? Stepping down to the road, it was with some satisfaction that I noticed 'THE RUSTY GUN' clearly marked on the bus stop sign. As the doors closed, I could hear 'Sorry, oops, so sorry' as the laundry basket lady made her way to my vacated seat.

It's over three hours since I left home, and I'm happy to finally set out on the trail. Twenty miles to St Albans will be a challenge, but there are opportunities to finish sooner. The path is flat and undemanding, so it's a mystery why my irregular heartbeat makes an early and unwelcome appearance; maybe it was the stress of the bus journey, or perhaps just bad luck. It gets a bit better, but after a couple of miles, it's much worse, and I have to sit under a tree and weigh up the options. As I'm doing so, and taking the opportunity to drink some water, I receive a text from an old friend: 'How are you?' it starts.

There is the possibility of catching a bus in the next village. But instead, I carry on, facing a taxing climb to an open, deserted hilltop. Struggle on for another six miles and get to Codicote, any thoughts of going further dispelled by the stiff ascent into the village centre. Two buses serve the community, one I just missed, but the other is due any minute. I looked up as another Hopper bus trundled up the hill. The young lady driver was far more welcoming and, better still, she knew the way to Stevenage Station.

Codicote to Redbourn: 29 July 2022 (18 miles)

Last week was a somewhat woeful wander. 'Circumstances beyond my control' meant I could only complete eight of the intended 20 miles. Today was perfect for a long walk, sunny but not too hot, pleasant countryside, interesting places, and feeling well. My plan is to get to St Albans and possibly beyond.

There were so many interesting places (POI, we'll call them) that the countryside may take a back seat, which is unfair because so much of it was delightful: field paths around golden crops, woodland paths, and more green lanes.

The first POI was Ayot St Lawrence, home to George Bernard Shaw and the ruins of St Lawrence Church. But not ruins that have come about by decay, neglect, or damage by conflict. This was a deliberate act of destruction. In 1776, the local squire had the church demolished, or as much of it as he could get away with before the bishop stopped him. His actions were not born out of idealism or a passion for sweeping out the past and heralding in the new but because the church spoilt the view from his new house.

However, he provided a replacement church in a field a little further north. It is built in neo-classical style, with Doric columns holding up an ostentatiously large porch. This front entrance was for the squire and his guests only. The rest of the village had to go round the back. A mausoleum on each side of the building is connected by more columns and lintels. One contains the remains of the squire and, in the other, his wife. Apparently, after a lifetime together, they wished to be parted in death.

We must return to the first century BC for our next POI, to the time when Julius Caesar paid us a visit. Just outside Wheathampstead is The Devil's Dyke, a prehistoric earthwork defence that has left a wide ditch through the woods. An inscription on a stone by the entrance gate tells that Caesar may have defeated the English king Cassivellaunus here in 54 BC. Whether or not he did, the walk through the sunken path, arched by a canopy of trees, still had an eerie feel.

Only a little further on is the town of Sandridge. I could have visited the oldest church in Hertfordshire; the path went through the churchyard, but I crossed the road to the pub instead. It was warm, and I fancied a pint to accompany my ham and cheese baguette. The landlord tried to put me off by warning me that my chosen lager was very expensive, but I decided to buy it anyway. He enthusiastically told of a Roman wall being restored in the beer garden. Apparently, a specialist firm had been working on it for many months, but this was their last week. I took my beer outside and chose a table beside an already finished section. It was a very nice wall.

The last three miles into St Albans passed through the model village of Childwick Green (model as in ideal rather than miniature). Built for farm workers on the local estate in the 19th century. A track around the edge of a large scorched field led down into the city.

St Albans is such an important POI that I won't attempt a description. Still, I did have a decision to make as I drank my deferred flask of tea, sitting on a bench opposite the entrance to the Roman Verulamium Museum. I could leave the route here and follow a path of just over a mile to the Abbey Station or follow the River Ver for five miles to Redbourn, where I hoped to catch a bus to Hemel Hempstead. If you've followed my previous adventures, you won't be surprised to hear I chose to go on.

Two miles from Redbourn, a bridge across the river was closed, deemed dangerous, with more missing planks than intact ones. My weary legs left me in no doubt that I was to ignore the diversion signs, promising in return to provide enough strength to climb over the inadequate plastic cordons and take my chances.

Take 18 trouble-free miles, add a few extra letters, and a woeful wander becomes a wonderful wander. Perfect.

Redbourn to Tring: 3 August 2022 (17 miles)

A short bus ride from Luton Station gets me back to Redbourn and the start of the last section of this long-distance path. An easy start on a short section of the Nickey Line – a disused railway running between Hemel Hempstead and Harpenden, previously met on the last section of the Chiltern Way.

Soon turning onto a wide track leading downhill through farmland and open countryside, Flamstead Church can be seen in the distance, and it's where we're headed. The village is somewhere else I visited on the Chiltern Way. However, the 'FLAMSTEAD' sign now has the addition of a woolly cover, similar to the post-box toppers prevalent today, but done in a grey weave that looks like chainmail and is slightly foreboding. For some reason it reminds me of the film *The Wicker Man*, but that seems a bit unfair on the residents of this lovely village. The rest of the morning takes a meandering path through rolling arable land displaying swathes of ripe crops, interspersed with more villages and narrow lanes.

Thinking it's time for lunch, I want to make sure my last stop on the Hertfordshire Way is a good one, especially as it's such a nice day. I shun various options in search of the perfect spot. I'm beginning to think I'll have to make do with anywhere I can sit down when the path opens up to a stunning hilltop view with a vacant bench to enjoy it. How annoying would it have been to stop a few minutes earlier and then pass this lovely provision?

Towards the end of the day, the route crosses the Ashridge Estate. Dropping down into the Golden Valley (a Capability Brown creation) and back up to pass the imposing Ashridge House. This enormous building with its abundance of castellations is apparently an example of Gothic Revival Architecture. The route passes the front door on its way to the Princes Drive which is a broad and straight grassy path that runs for a mile to the Bridgewater Memorial and the National Trust car park.

It's a hot afternoon, and when I see an ice-cream van, I can't resist. 'Large cone, please,' I say to the driver. 'What flavour do you want then?' he asks a little grumpily. (Should grumpy ice-cream sales personnel be allowed?) 'Vanilla,' I reply, as if there could be any other choice. I also requested a Diet Coke, but he only had the ordinary kind. I accept this, arguing that I need the sugar hit for the last few miles. I hadn't tasted an ordinary Coke for several years and looked forward to the experience. It could remind me of my childhood when a vending machine delivered ice-cold Pepsi into a plastic cup. But I was disappointed. It was sweet and syrupy. I must have become too accustomed to the preferred alternative.

Another mile through a descending tree-lined path until meeting up with the Ridgeway National Trail. Together, we tackled a steep woodland path, then a narrow, hedge-enclosed footpath to Tring Station, where my 195-mile journey ends.

Mixed emotions at finishing: pleasure at the achievement but sadness that it's over. Before this year, the Hertfordshire Way was a casual acquaintance, met only when another route occasionally shared a mile or two along the same path. Now, it's more like an old friend, and I shall miss its meandering route and reassuring waymarkers. Paradoxically, I shall also miss the anticipation of not knowing what's around the next bend – even an unwelcome hill climb holds the promise of a stunning vista (although seldom does).

So, where to go next? Time to get the maps out and start planning. Give me a couple of weeks, and I'll think of something.